I AM MY FATHER'S DAUGHTER

A COLLECTION OF STORIES ABOUT FATHER-DAUGHTER RELATIONSHIPS

EDITED BY

JANETH A. BENJAMIN

CONTENTS

INTRODUCTION

Welcome to the I am My Father's Daughter Anthology. This collection is a kaleidoscope of emotions and experiences about one of the most important parental relationships in our lives. The idea to publish this collection was birthed in the middle of the 2020 pandemic. As the submissions came in, I got nervous. Undertaking a task such as this came with hurdles but with the most understanding group of supporters, came real stories, about real experiences, a true testament to how connected we are despite location, age, race, social or cultural background.

This is a global experience starting in Bronx and journeying through moments, memories, and lessons. The most common questions asked about this project was if the stories were only about the good times. The answer is no. There is a balance as they mirror the complexities and joys of father-daughter relationships. The journey to becoming despite any ups and downs and in-betweens. The contributors examined and accepted how instrumental the relationships with their fathers have been to their growth and healing. The stories connect rather than divide. They inspire and empower, but most importantly they allow us to reflect on a key relationship that has shaped our identity.

I hope that you enjoy the stories but also celebrate the bravery of the women[1] telling their stories in their way. Our journey to becoming the best versions of ourselves requires acceptance, celebration, and authenticity.

---

[1] Contributor, Jenny Nash identifies as non-binary; They have no issues with the use of women in this context.

THEO'S LEGACY

Janeth A. Benjamin
The Bronx, New York

"You need to keep the Kingdom of yourself and your temple in a position where you can function and serve your purpose"

Evon Theodore Benjamin, 2020

The older I got, the more I was able to recognize the parts of my personality that were like a particular parent. My father is grossly misunderstood, especially by the people around him or think they know him. I don't know his story but the one thing he has been passionate about is health. When you meet him, he will give the chicken-hormone lecture. Or scold you for mixing your fruits. He tested and concluded that fruit smoothies have been causing mucus buildup leading to frequent colds. As it was better to consume fruits separate from proteins allowing a 30-minute window for digestion. My father boasted going years without catching a cold, a foolproof method he's been living by since around the seventies or so. But that's not the only thing he will be known for. His children are an important part of this journey and I only know a smidgen of that story.

My brother Krishna posted this on his Instagram account, and I had to borrow it *"You need to keep the Kingdom of yourself and your temple in a position where you can function and serve your purpose"*. Daddy wrote it. Our father has never been a regular father. I recall his absence for many periods of my life, but he showed up at some of the most important times. My mother despite her heartbreak never spoke poorly of him to us and allowed him to still be in our lives. My father has six children, I am the second oldest. My brother Daniel and I were born in the same year, four months apart.

When I was about seventeen years old, I asked him about what happened between him, and my mother and he quickly told me that it was none of my business. I argued that I was a unique product of the relationship, so I have at least a stake in its demise. He still did not disclose. Truth be told, my mother spared no details. Her broken moments, the happy moments, and the time my grandmother referred to her as <u>*"that girl"*</u> in a letter to him. My father's mother was a school principal, her siblings were professionals as well. My mother's parents worked odd jobs to make ends meet. So, my father's decision to be with my mother was unacceptable. But my father was a rebel. He did what he wanted, when he wanted because everything was about his purpose, his calling, his legacy.

In my second year of college, he got me a job at his workplace. My interview was basically chit-chatting with the claims department manager, his supervisor. The week I started working, I was recovering from a bout of pneumonia leading to an asthma diagnosis, and confirmation that I was anemic. That Friday was my last appointment following my course of antibiotics. He offered to take me back to the campus and we got into a rather heated discussion about my health. A conversation that had been happening since I was a teen. He was rather annoyed that I wanted to eat more liver and not greens for my anemia. He had been a vegan since the seventies and in tip-top shape, so no one was spared his passion for eating healthy. Like most of our "arguments", respect and the decision to disagree amicably left us laughing about something. In a strange twist, he started telling me about some of his younger years leading up to why he chose my mother. After college, he got a job in Kingston and traveled on a scooter daily around the treacherous junction road from St. Mary. One morning, a tree fell across the road in front of him and he said his life flashed across his face. He had nothing to leave, he had no legacy.

My father and I don't have a 'normal' father-daughter relationship. But we have a connection. He is not the cuddly type, but he shows his affection his way. I would get random timely phone calls or emails mostly encouraging me to take care of myself. He even offered once to raise my unborn children, should I ever have them. His legacy was having children. I applaud my mother and stepmothers for not injecting a world of hate in his children's hearts for him. He is by far without faults. But he will always be daddy. The only two times I lived with him was before I turned five and my memories of each time are still very vivid. The first time it was with him, my stepmother Sophia and uncle Tony. The second time with my sister Levonne, Auntie Sophia and my brother Krishna who was just a baby. We had a home in Irish Town, a golden retriever, and a peach tree in the front of the yard. But we missed our mother so, words were said, and we were disciplined. I remember hating cod liver oil pills and that I hid them in a corner in the dining room.

Although I was raised by my mother and grandmother, I always knew who my father was. Getting to know my father meant letting go of all the conventional things about fatherhood. He never subscribed to stereotypes and laughed at those who did. His intelligence is natural, and I glimpsed his charm when we worked together.

His concern now is still about my health, and I finally get it. It took some years of lecturing, but I finally got what the big deal was about taking care of yourself. He knew and tried his hardest to help me understand. I think we are all at that place where we can proudly say daddy wasn't all that crazy. But only because we understand his level of crazy since we are just as crazy. I marvel at the wonder of genetics and how we were all crafted with traits so spot on.

There is simply no denying that the apple didn't fall from the tree. Except these apples have been bearing fruit and continue to bear fruit because of one decision he made over thirty something years ago. Maybe one day I will get the entire story, regrets, and all, but for now, I am keeping the kingdom of myself and temple in a position where I can function and serve my purpose.

THE MICKEY MOUSE TURNOVER CHOO-CHOO TRAIN

Cher Finver
Las Vegas, Nevada

In the decade of bell bottoms and disco, Disney released the Mickey Mouse Turnover Choo-Choo. The train station revolved while Goofy held his suitcase, and Donald Duck reminded you to slow down. The bright yellow train track would turn over by the engine's weight with Mickey as the conductor, sending him back the way he came. Minnie, Pluto, and one of Donald's nephews were present, in the form of a sticker, waving along the track. I never felt that big of an attachment to this train, even though it was one of my first toys. I do remember the children on the box looked way too thrilled. Perhaps they were pretending as I did that their childhoods were happy ones.

The train was a gift from my father. That could explain my impartial feelings. It also most likely explains the hidden desire I had to always tuck the train away safely in a moving box. Making sure wherever I went, it went. It was, after all, the only reminder of my father I had. At some point, the moving box selected to protect it mistakenly made its way to Goodwill.

Parental alienation. If you are not familiar with the term, I envy you. Wikipedia states, "Parental alienation describes a process through which a child becomes estranged from a parent as the result of the psychological manipulation of another parent." I wrote a memoir in 2017, *But You Look So Good and Other Lies*. In part, my book goes into greater detail regarding the manipulation of me by the person who was supposed to protect me the most. That would be my mother. Against whom, I only now know to be, my well-meaning father.

Let me save you from dropping a few bucks on my book. I grew up with stories that my father was a "mean man who did mean things." When I was nine, Dad tried to obtain more visitations with me. My mother told me I'd be ripped from her and my only brother at the time and never see them again. When I was ten, my brother and I thought we were heading to Hershey Park in PA. Days later, we ended up in Las Vegas, NV. I knew that was a long way from our home, family, and friends on Long Island, NY. You can imagine my shock and the subsequent trauma I experienced when I realized Vegas was now our home.

I felt the weight on my young adolescent shoulders as we moved from one seedy apartment to another every six months or so. Attending different schools, so my dad could not locate me. Even though growing up, all I heard was that my dad had little desire to see me. And that he never paid child support while my other siblings' dads paid theirs. There were also stories that he bit me and threw pots and pans at me whenever I would cry.

A child believes what a mother tells them. In the faint memories I did have of my dad, stepmom, and stepsister, there were flashes of pool parties and delicious Strawberry Nesquik mix in the tin container. I always doubted those memories. And my sanity. I would find out later in life through therapy that this harmful behavior is what you call gaslighting.

I would also grow to realize that my mother was flawed (aren't we all?) and selfish. She'd choose the local casino and their endless free drinks over quality time with her children. She preferred men over her children too. I will ruin more of my book by telling you that my mother lied to me about my father. Documents and a long line of relatives have confirmed that. I wasn't asking many questions as a child or young adult. I wish I would have been brave enough too. Distant relatives didn't know what I knew as a child and felt it wasn't their place to pull me aside. Fair enough.

That stepsister I mentioned. Five years ago, we found each other on Facebook. That would lead to conversations with my stepmom and my father. We started with, "So, what is your favorite color and movie?" Questions one already should have been able to answer about the other. During our first few calls, I found out the full extent of my mother's lies and self-serving agenda. My dad has receipts for child support payments dating back to the late 70s and early 80s. I was not aware that he would show up for a scheduled visit, and my mother would lie, claiming I was sick. I was also unaware that the judge reprimanded my mom for continually bringing my dad to court to increase his child support.

In recent years, an aunt relayed a story that may explain some of my mother's indifferent feelings toward me. Mom wanted me only after seeing the attention that her brother and his wife were receiving as they were expecting. When Mom accomplished her goal, she picked the "perfect" time to announce the news. As the guest entered the church for my brand-new cousin's christening, Mom blocked the entrance, leading hands to touch her belly as family and friends tried to maneuver to their seats. My mother would end up cheating on my father and leave him for my little brother's dad when I was two.

It has been years since I spoke to or seen the woman who birthed me. The family rift has unfortunately claimed the relationship with some of my siblings as a casualty. Family dinners, time together at the holidays, I do miss it. It's just me, my husband, and our daughter most of the time nowadays. My mother owns a home twenty minutes from me, but she might as well live in a different country.

I spoke to my dad every other week for a full year before we reunited in person. I happened to be in New York City for work and took the train from Jamaica to Ronkonkoma the next morning. I felt excitement, not nerves, as I stared out the gritty window waiting for my stop. When I finally got to hug my dad, neither of us wanted to let go.

My dad, stepmom, stepsister, and I have rebuilt our relationship one phone call, one Facebook interaction, and one visit at a time. I also didn't realize I have an aunt and cousin on my dad's side too. They live closer to me in Arizona, and I try to visit once or twice a year. My aunt and stepmom fuss over me, and I'll admit I'm not used to that from a maternal parental figure. Not since my grandmother died anyway.

I always arrive at my aunt's house to the aroma of a home-cooked meal. My stepmom once insisted on having my dad drive us around in the pouring rain so I could enjoy my favorite New York cheese pizza and garlic bagels. My stepsister and I sometimes enjoy cordial liquors or Moscato. My dad and stepmom always have these spirits purchased long before I knock on their door. I genuinely appreciate these small acts of kindness, which simply show they care.

During the COVID-19 pandemic, online shopping, or at least adding wish-list items to my cart, has been a frequent activity. I had cut myself off from eBay in the early 2000s after I found myself hiding packages from UPS. But last week, I found myself back on the site, just looking. Then, it dawned on me! I hit search after typing, "Disney toy train." I'm scrolling down until I'm not. There it is! That 70s orange box, those damn happy children. I hit "Buy It Now."

Possessing this childhood toy again brings me such joy and a reminder that I was loved by my dad my entire life. He tried to find me and fight for me. I know that now. My dad does not hold a grudge against my mother. "We go from here," he says. I admire his grace.

My insane lifetime love of all things Disney? It had to start with my train! I visit Disneyland at least once a year. And yes, I'm one of *those* people who get teary when they see the castle. It is my wish that one day, I can visit a Disney Park with my dad. Maybe we can ride the train off into the suns.

HE LOVED ME FIRST

Eleanor Sevigny
Galesburg, Illinois

The day I was born was not an ordinary day for my dad. My dad was in his mid-thirties when he met my mom. By then, he was convinced that he would never have a family. After they got married, he and my mom started trying to conceive a child. Each miscarriage brought them both pain. When they finally carried a baby to term and thought that they were going to have that child that they wanted so badly, my mom was diagnosed with preeclampsia. Her pregnancy ended in an emergency cesarean, with both my life and hers on the line. At that moment, my dad felt like he was going to lose everything. Why had he tried for more? He should've been happy with what he had. Now he was going to lose the family he had dreamed of having. I had swallowed my meconium – this required immediate medical treatment after my birth. When my dad finally got to hold me for the first time, the child he always wanted to hold but thought he would never get the chance to; it was love at first sight. That first meeting has forever described our relationship. He loved me from the moment he first saw me. He was there for me from the moment I was born.

As a little girl, I loved going for rides around the family farm in my dad's farm truck. These rides always meant quality time with him and a chance to visit my grandparents, who lived on the other side of the farm. One of the times I was sitting in my dad's truck as we drove around the farm, I heard the song I loved Her First by Heartland for the first time. I knew that song would be the song I danced to with my dad at my wedding. The lyrics described the whole-hearted love I felt from my dad every moment of every day. There was never a time when I doubted that he loved me. He loved and supported me from the day I was born and always would.

He showed me this in many ways. One way was when I was in middle school. My middle school was different from others. Seventh and eighth-grade classes were combined. I easily made friends in these classes, but most of them were a year ahead of me. This was not a problem until I was in eighth grade. Most of my friends had moved on to high school. Leaving me alone and an easy target for bullying. The bullying I dealt with at school led to depression. My dad readily listened to my struggles whenever I was willing to speak about them and encouraged me to talk to a teacher. When I finally opened to one of my favorite teachers, she immediately took me to the principal and handled the situation. My dad congratulated me at home for being brave enough to ask for help and confront a hard situation.

Another way he showed me how much he loved me was the extra time we spent together while my mom took my siblings to 4-H and tutoring. Once my dad came home from work, we would go on father-daughter shopping dates. We didn't always buy something, but we would drive around town, look at the salvage shops, used cars, etc.... and talk. I knew that for as long as he lived, he would be there for me. He would love me.

As I've gotten older and started my own family, that love never changed. When I wanted to join a church that he was not a part of, he encouraged me to follow my heart. The day my mom refused to let me get married unless I met her criteria, he told me to do what makes me happy. I followed his advice and married my husband. On my wedding day, my dad and I danced to *I Loved Her First* by Heartland, just like I always knew we would. There was not a dry eye at the reception.

Years later, the first time I was going to tell him he would be a grandfather, he answered his cellphone while putting new shingles on the roof of his house. I elected not to tell him that day. I'm glad I waited because when I told him he was going to be a grandfather, I'm pretty sure he would've fallen off the roof with excitement if I had told him the day before. You could feel the happiness and love in his voice as he congratulated me.

Since then, I call him whenever I need parenting advice. Especially the first time one of my kids was sick. I knew the basics of what to do (I had taken care of myself as a sick adult), but I wanted confirmation that I was doing the right thing. There was no question on who to talk to. I called my dad. Check her temperature regularly, push fluids, use a damp washcloth on her forehead to help her body regulate its temperature, use a nasal aspirator to help clear her nose of mucus, and call him back if things get worse or she gets better. On days when I feel like I'm drowning in motherhood (like when my toddler pooped in her diaper, stuck her hands in her diaper, and proceeded to coat herself and everything around her in it), I call him to vent or in a lot of cases laugh about how kids can be kids.

I know that most women have this kind of relationship with their mom, but my mom and I have never been that close. It's always been my dad and me. I think that started when I was in middle school. As I've mentioned before my siblings were tutored by a specialist, so my mom was constantly driving them to tutoring appointments and school. When she was not doing that, she was driving them to 4-H activities. This left me on my own a lot with my dad. On a typical day, I would ride the bus home from school, walk home from the bus stop, eat a snack, and do my homework. After my homework was done, I would wait for dad to get home. I would always hear his truck coming before I saw it. The crunch of his tires on the gravel was very distinct. When dad got home, he'd take care of the animals. At the time we had two goats, chickens, four cats, and a dog. Depending on the day, he would also need to drive the trash across the farm to be ready for pickup at the loading dock. Once he'd taken care of all the chores, he'd take a shower marking the end of his chores and the workday. Then we'd talk, watch the news together, go for a drive, go shopping, make dinner, etc.… Those years, my formative years as a woman were spent with my dad.

He didn't shame me for becoming a woman. Periods were not something gross, they were part of life. If I was too shy or embarrassed to buy my menstrual products, he would buy them for me. I remember one day my period started early while I was at school. I called him on my cell phone, and he used his lunch break to bring me a paper bag with pads in it as I asked. I was touched when I took the bag. He had taken the time to find something that would hide what he was giving me. He knew I was self-conscious about my period even though I didn't need to be. After he left, I rushed to the bathroom. I wanted to replace the makeshift pad I had made of a bunch of the rough public school toilet paper stuffed into my underwear with something less likely to leak and more comfortable. When I opened the bag, my heart swelled with the knowledge of how much my dad loved and paid attention to me. Even though I didn't ask, he had included ibuprofen in the bag because he knew I always had horrible cramps. Years later, when my periods became so bad that they were causing me to hemorrhage, I didn't have to worry about what my dad would do. He took me to urgent care. The doctor recommended a prescription for birth control,

I never had to experience that again. He didn't question what I would use the prescription for. He didn't shame me for my needs. He made sure I was taken care of.

I'm very blessed. My dad showed me what a man should be like. He showed me that toxic masculinity had no place in my life. That if a man could not accept everything that being a woman entailed, he was not worth my time.

Yes, he loved me first, and I'm glad he did.

UNMASKED, ME

Natalie Carroll
Scotland

My story never gets easier to talk about; it only gets easier to deal with. Do you know the meaning of loss? I believe it's being stripped away of all you've ever known, the people, the places, the memories, and the happiness. Loss, it's a powerful feeling. It's the next saddest feeling right after love. It seizes the moment, and at that moment, it can break you like no other feeling can. It leaves you feeling angry, hurt, and confused. It can also send someone into a spiral of depression—it can make you feel useless—your search for any reason to comprehend. But can any good come from trying to understand what it is to lose all that you love?

He's been gone so long now it's as if he never really existed. That the only place he did exist was my mind - much like an imaginary friend. That's what the memories remind me of. And yet, I've always had this perfect idea of what the perfect life would be like. It would be the feeling of always knowing I would have him. And he would always want me. I wanted that feeling that I know I'm making him happy. Knowing I'm making him proud of me. But that's the disappointing part; he'll never know me. I know my perfect life, but I am flawed. I'm not a dependable person when things get hard … I run - it's all I've ever known. Ironically, the apple doesn't fall far from the tree. It's been eighteen, maybe nineteen years, since my father left me.

Seven years old, I have a family and friends, a beautiful life that I did indeed cherish. But some part of me has always felt lost. Almost as though I was filled with the emptiness within myself. Hollow. That's what it felt like to always have this void within me: almost like an astronaut without his rocket, floating aimlessly in space, I had been stripped of my emotions, yet I was so overwhelmed by everything; I shut off and became unable to feel anything but guilt and blame. But that's when I found the gravitation that pulled me back down. The moment I learned I wasn't enough for my father. He didn't want me. He didn't want anything to do with me. To me in my eyes, that's when I lost my father. It all must have been too much for him to learn he was going to be a father again. It must have been terrifying, dreadful, maybe even disappointing. So, to fill the void, he picked his high fuming substances over his own child. A drug or two to hijack his system, to mix in with his alcoholic binge every other day of the week. But it didn't matter, right? Because I was just a money bank, right? It doesn't matter because I was only his first daughter. After I moved on with my life, I found out he cherished me, by replacing me with another daughter. That was now his little girl instead of me. So, I guess it didn't matter, right? I have a couple of memories of him, but they aren't happy ones. For a long time, I always thought that I was the problem. I searched and searched for any means necessary to find an answer.

But I never could find one. To find an answer - so I could stop making excuses, for why my father didn't love me enough to be in my life. Maybe even stop blaming myself. The sad part is, I always thought it was my fault that he turned to drugs when I was born.

I have always felt as though I was in a big swirl of darkness, knowing that the only person I wanted in my life wasn't here with me. It left me heartbroken. To know someone, you looked up to as your hero who doesn't want anything to do with you kills a person inside so many times. Especially when you're their flesh and blood, the betrayal runs through your veins, gradually turning thinner than water. Then comes the crippling self-doubt when you begin to question your very existence, which can never prepare you for a wound like mine. "Does he think of me as a mistake, a regret?" "Am I?" And I tortuously question, "Am I the reason why he left my mum and me?

Isn't it ironic, despite his intentions? Every year on my birthday I would make the same wish. I used to wish for my father to change his mind and love me as his child. Whenever it was Christmas, I used to think as a kid that if I was good enough all year round, then Santa would grant me my one wish, for my father to want to be in my life. But time went on, and I got older; that's when I lost hope in the idea. Waiting for my wishes to come true was like waiting for a drought in the Sahara Desert, pointless and disappointing.

I was seven years old when I learned some people are like butterflies; they only stay for a while. It took me until I was about twenty - three maybe even twenty-four to realize why I had so much resentment, why I have so much anger and why I still have questions. I understand what I went through made me who I am, but I just want to know why I had to go through it? I guess that was back in a time where I could feel my heart silently breaking… how I know, because I was the only one who could hear it. I wish someone who was absent most of my life didn't affect me. But it does, I still care. I care a lot. And I still care! So, I grew up coping with the mystery of absence and let down. I've had to armor myself with a sense of survival: coping, without time and distance to heal. I've had to learn as I got older that nobody told you how to feel and that life doesn't come with an instruction manual.

When I was sixteen years old, my life spiraled out of control. I had become addicted to a drug. Indulging myself in the drug I had been taking became my crutch, I depended on it. My problem was not only addiction but also sheer naivety; I believed everything the packet promised to deliver. From the moment you start taking this drug you forget. You gave it direct permission to mess with your thoughts, so much you lose sight of the person you were. You slowly start to deteriorate as a person and become almost unrecognizable.

Nevertheless, it gives you such a rush; the type of rush you get after you come off a roller coaster. The adrenaline courses through your veins, leaving you with such a high! That makes you feel almost invincible. But when you stop taking it…you realize going through withdrawal that none of the promises that are on the packet are delivered. Your trust is snapped like a twig, yet you persist in taking the drug. No one tells you to love works like a drug, making you delusional, so much so, you become in denial with the side effects. I guess that's where my problems stem from. I wasn't aware at the time, but I was left with an ever-lasting effect. I became much like an ice cube, within my preserved self—cold, hard, and numb. Fast-forward a couple of months later, I booked myself into my rehab.

The first step wasn't about putting my hands up and admitting I had a problem but simply facing my problem. However, little did I know I was, and l always have been my hero? Instead of sitting waiting and looking around hopefully for a white knight in shining armor or even a superman to swoop in and save me. I've always been the one who gave myself that self-assurance. I never knew how strong I was until I had to forgive someone who wasn't sorry and accept an apology I never received. It took me a long time to understand what it means to forgive someone. Always wondered how I could forgive someone who chose to hurt me. But after a lot of soul searching, I realized that forgiveness isn't about accepting or excusing their behavior…It is about letting it go and preventing their behavior from destroying my heart.

Whenever I would ask about my father as a young kid I was told "he does love you just in his way." What does that exactly mean? Does it mean that he only loves you when he has something to gain from you? Or does it mean he's someone who can love you desperately with their feelings and still not know how to love you correctly with their actions, is that why he walked away? It doesn't stop me from wondering if he loved me. Does he regret walking away? Is there a chest of drawer with written letters that he has always wanted to post but just couldn't bring himself to do so? Does he even have any memories he looks over about me? Did he always secretly wish me a happy birthday I didn't know about?

The only thing I am sure of is this, I'm like a shattered mug. I'm broken. There are too many pieces and not enough glue to fix it. It doesn't help that there are even some pieces missing. If I were to describe myself in one sentence it would be that I am a jumbled puzzle but a beautiful mess in disguise. Maybe that's why I can be compared to a Rubik's cube. What hurts the most is people don't hurt you, your expectations do. Eventually, you learn the more you care the more you leave yourself to become vulnerable. So, I learned to stop letting people get close.

Instead, I don't hesitate to cut people off. I don't trust someone to get close to me. I don't trust them to stay…I trust them to leave and kick the scattered pieces of my heart as they walk away. It saves you from playing a game of chess to know someone's intentions for you. What happens when you get caught up in the fairy-tale? What happens when you find someone who makes you feel complete? What happens when you shape your life around them and then it all falls apart? What are you supposed to do then? Perhaps that's why I find it easy to suppress my emotions. That way you can avoid someone leaving you, hurting, or cheating on you. Besides, it's always the people you either love or idolize who hurt you in the end.

DIALED IN

MacKenzie Miller
Portland, Oregon

I could tell something was wrong about 30 seconds into the phone call. My excitement fell on dead air, static-filled my ears instead of a voice. As it rang through, my end of the line seemed to increase in weight by the moment. Daddy's voice, one that was *always* piercing and bold, had shrunk to this infinitesimal whisper that I'd never known to cross his lips. I didn't realize it at the time, but that phone call would be the beginning of the rest of my life-changing shape. The pinnacle moment of togetherness, the last time I would foster a complete, unbroken family unit within my heart.

My father had always been described by my friends growing up as intimidating. Standing 6'4" and typically toting a scowl, I could see why they might think that. I was even often intimidated by his stature. When he was mad, an entire city block could have felt the tension that was often confined to our quaint three-bedroom home. I can count on both my hands the number of times the man had smiled for a photo while I was growing up and still have a few fingers left over. His gaze was enough to silence you, but if the situation demanded it, his booming voice would stop you in your tracks. This isn't to say we had a difficult relationship while I was young, but to set the tone for my upbringing, you'd have to know these things. I can still hear echoes of his laugh ringing around the living room when I'd shout a horribly wrong answer to a Jeopardy question with such conviction, still feel an arm wrap around me as he told me quietly how proud he was of me after he'd been dragged along to one of many band concerts he'd have just as happily not attended. I've always known my father loved me, but it was always just distant, always slightly out of reach.

The day I made that phone call, though, all of that changed. I had bounced excitedly up and down in the passenger seat of my then-fiancé's late 90s Volvo sedan, a new shiny ring on the fourth finger of my left hand. My glee was not equally matched on the other end of the call as my father relayed information to me that I didn't know now would be the start of a long hard dredge through a divorce. While I shared the news a few days later with close friends, they all told me how happy I should be that it didn't happen when I was younger. How happy I should be that I didn't have to worry about custody battles and dividing my school vacations and holiday schedules between two opposing parents who shared a love and a home and a family for so many years but who now can't stand to be in the same space with the other. How happy I should be that I was an adult going through this, that I don't have to worry.

Sure, they were right. I didn't have to worry about making sure I had two sets of everything so I could split time between two homes while going through school. I didn't have to worry if I was going to my mom's house for spring break and spending summer with dad. But the idea of this being easy crossing their minds was downright comical. Being an adult dealing with divorce meant I was flung into unfiltered chaos. I was completely grasping the gravity of everything going on around me and being stable enough to rely on to get through it. My father had always been a strong, ominous presence in my life—someone who loved, but in an almost guarded way. Someone who faced challenges stubbornly, never backing down. And to see him in this uncharted territory was startling. Like he was suddenly submerged in a vast body of water trying like hell to stay afloat with no sight of the shore, and I became his life raft.

This would become an entirely new experience for me. Being the assistance instead of needing assistance from a parent is a topsy turvy roller coaster ride, but it ultimately landed me so much closer to my father. Instead of being distant and just out of reach, he was now always beside me. I became not only a daughter, but a personal assistant, a schedule keeper, and most importantly, a confidant. Where in the past, my father had kept all his troubles locked away deep within himself—never uttering them to anyone I don't think, much less to his young daughter—I was now facing an onslaught of emotions I never knew my father could carry. Worry turned hair white; fear ebbed at the large man he had been until he was thinner than me resembling a shell of the figure used to tower over me. But instead of standing by while watching him struggle to carry a load of all these new challenges alone, I stood beside him and shouldered as much as I could carry to ease the burden. I could feel relief wash through the space we occupied together as he began to place his trust in me.

We carried on this way for months, him and I side by side trudging through the trenches of the disaster that was bestowed onto him. Each passing day brought us a little closer. I want to reiterate that my father was never unloving. He always told me goodnight, and he would be there for soccer games even though he hated listening to other parents scream at their children to do better. We had just always been ever so slightly out of touch with one another. But while weathering the storm of unexpected and uninhibited change together, my father and I have formed a relationship that transcends father and daughter. The man who was always just at arm's reach now envelopes me in a hug as soon as I see him, and again before leaving, and probably several times between those two moments. The man who raised me with a gruff voice and stern looks now boasts a laugh as large as he stands and smiles for photos. The man that I grew up with as my daddy is now a man, I call one of my best friends.

SMITTEN AND FULL OF GRATITUDE

Dianne R. Scott
Dover, Delaware

"I am a princess not because I have a prince, but because my father is a king" Unknown

In August 1944, a little chocolate baby boy was born. He'd taken the streets of Suffolk, VA, by storm with a legendary corniness before relocating to Delaware at 13 years old. It was then and where he met the adolescent young lady who would come to be his wife. Together, within their 53 years of marriage and counting…they'd beget five daughters and share 'grandparenthood' of eight grandchildren.

My father and I were fingernail biters. One of my earliest recollections, I remember, is saying rather sassily, "I bite my fingernails like my Daddy!" as I happily gnawed away. My mother said that I was about three years old at the time. My father also used to smoke cigarettes. At a very early age, I recall loving the smell of his stark white T-shirts that were scented with Newport cigarettes and the clean, fresh smell of washed laundry. I think back to the time he took our dog's puppies to the SPCA because we couldn't keep the ones left after giving some away in the neighborhood. He returned home with them because he just couldn't find it in his heart to leave them away from all that they knew in their young lives. I thought he was so sweet. My mother, sisters, and I attended church regularly, but some Sundays, Daddy, did too. Mommy would cornrow his hair the night before, and it produced THE best afro in the morning! I was one impressed little girl! And his eyes. One day, I rode my tricycle down the street to the little lady's house I loved to visit.

While eating the never-ending supply of butterscotch candy she kept in the pocket of her house dress, we chatted about what little old ladies liked to chat about with little girls who loved to chat - but I didn't realize I'd been gone for so long until I could hear my mother cry my name out... Dianne...?! Quickly, I beckoned my fellow chatter goodbye and hastily pedaled back up the street towards Mommy's voice - and then there they were. Daddy's eyes. I can still them - an emotionally charged bright brown (they turn that color with anger) yet unmistakably filled with worry as well as relief. Oh, I knew I was in trouble - the streetlights were on! - but his eyes still made me feel warm and loved. At any rate, I can only think that as early as that, I was smitten with my Daddy. And it never went away.

Daddy was also instrumental in teaching us how ladies should - and should not - be treated. His most powerful example was (is), as a husband, the unconditional love, adoration, respect, and loyalty he felt and showed our mother was superlative, and he didn't stop there. He demonstrates the very same for my sisters and me. He loved hard, was fiercely protective, let us know through words and deeds that we deserved, shouldn't accept nor expect anything less. Some examples of what emanated from such influence were: potential and selected suitors had to come correct or not come at all, the many thoughts/stories/lessons he shared and taught throughout the years which created within me the 'Daddy said...' syndrome, much to the chagrin of my friends, I was always the plus-sized sister, yet I always just knew and felt that I looked great, and folks far and near knew not to mess with Scotty's wife and five girls! But make no mistake, he was no pushover, not moved by (guilt) tears, and required his daughter's A-game, obedience, and respect - always. Falling short brought about consequences. Period. When I put forth my not-so-best effort in high school and brought home much less than stellar grades, he referred to my report card as "dog sh--" and grounded me until the next marking period. And that included no telephone privileges! Yes, he used expletives at times, but if he heard anyone else doing so, he was quick to advise them, "Hey...my daughters (and/or) wife are here!" and that was that. With that said, I remain smitten with my Daddy. And it'll never go away.

Growing up, my father may have been a bit rough around the edges in some ways. Still, my mother was always there with 'balance.' Together, they managed well with the loving parental task of providing an environment where little girls felt loved and safe, hence, blossoming into intelligent, strong, courageous, respectful, proud, self-sufficient young ladies and women. And it's no wonder why, when at the age of 37 and I faced the toughest situation, I'd ever faced, I did so courageously. I was diagnosed with Multiple Sclerosis, a chronic and often disabling (as in my case) disease of the brain and spinal cord (central nervous system) of which there's no cure at this juncture. I'm living a life with a plethora of challenges, and yet I feel safe, bold, and strong, with my main defense being positivity and the 'stuff that's in me.' My father did that; our relationship, coupled with the upbringing he (and my mother) provided, has been paramount in my ability to be the woman and mother I am today despite my health struggles. For the ever-loving, protective, and helpful nature that has always enveloped me, I am not only smitten, but I also have a wealth of gratitude.

He is witty, but he doesn't play. He's kind yet can be a tad edgy. He sings beautifully though that same voice can 'bark.' He may shy away from purchasing feminine products in the store. Yet, he valiantly served in the US Army as a paratrooper, fought in the Vietnam War, and received several commendations, including a purple heart. He is the epitome of strength, fiercely protective, gallant, proud, and lovable. 'He' is my father, my dad... 'He' is my Daddy. And I? I am the product of all that is him. *I Am My Father's Daughter*. And at 50 years old, I am as smitten with him today as that little girl of yesteryear.

MEMOIR OF THE ENDURING FILIAL SUPPORT

Archana Bahadur Zutshi
India

A soft, smooth fold of his bulky back to which I clung as a cocoon. On camelback, I was in tandem with the movement as his body sang the movement. My first infant impression of Dad's protective stance! That moment etched, and it became a static image of the wall he was. The metaphor and emblem of a noble Dad, holding us in good stead, fencing off the colossal impact of any crisis and offering us ebullience and spirited humor. A tragedy would just flicker by as we were under his constant light.

He was the rock. The great skies where cosmic interplay in bursts was evinced. I remember Sr Cabrini relating to the class how sacred the father-daughter relationship was. How gingerly she clasped her dad's hand as he lay dying. Something recreated for me, by the turn of the wheel, within the next three years. Our relationship too had that restraint due to both of us being quiet and observant.

Extraordinary fathers provide the right atmosphere to their daughters. One amazing quality about my dad was he never allowed any discriminatory remarks on a gender basis, undermining my capabilities. His presence was empowering. Not only my opinion mattered, but he gave lessons in life nuanced on his own. Indirectly, he vociferously sounded what was desirable in a situation and taught me a lot about discernment.

I am my father's daughter. His boldness and fearlessness gave me the streak of boldness. He was forthright. A disciplinarian with his children, but at the same time, he gave sufficient space to his progeny. His fierce guarding of truthfulness was exemplary.

One day he discovered his chair broken by one of us. We were interrogated by turns; since the guilty did not own up, we were given a rap in equal measure. A few days later, I broke his ballpen with multicolored refills, a gift. I was a bit alarmed.

"So, you fiddled with this pen?"

"Daddy, I did! Sorry!"

His anger subsided. Though he held the pen close to his heart, his expression altered. The much-anticipated punitive strike fizzled out in front of my discerning eye. Constant guidance by example and gentle pursuance was the characteristic of his interaction. He once told me about an extremely handsome young fellow in his college in the 1940s.

"That fellow misused his physical attractiveness … he finally became a pimp for prostitutes." His narrative held us spellbound as he related the incidents and stories with marked fervor. We listened in awe to the amazing anecdotes. His humor made the days burden-free. His ebullient spirit rubbed an optimism in the gathering. Fond of Urdu verses, he would render a few couplets from the ghazals, from his extensive readings.Some revolutionary thought, something which drove the entire nation. In his inimitable style, his cadenced, well-intoned poetic session, seemed captivating. Often, he got a request for an encore. His robust voice in high bass and trebles was very convincing. Often juxtaposition is employed by the poets, so well he effortlessly brought the caesura into focus.

Once I heard him recite by heart an Urdu ghazal (poem, may be set to music) by poet Iqbal. I could feel the rapture. Slowly I swirled the old wine, sipping the flavors which swept the nation in a tizzy to throw off the imperialist yoke of the British regime in India. My down on arms stood on end, such a fiery call for rebellion. Dying was not his fear, but a challenge to the crushing authority. The poet's impassioned plea for himself was

"We are consumed by the revolutionary zeal; Let's see against our endurance what power the murderous arm holds as the oppressor."

His eloquent delivery made me his great admirer. The idealism, zest for life evinced in the couplets he rendered made me see him as the paragon of human rights. He respected all without any bias.

My dad spoke less, but he was supportive of all I did. As a child, he would nudge my mother to let me have a pick from the array of garments. She would often joke that the father pampered the daughter with the most expensive dresses.

He was a movie buff. Whenever we could go, we were taken out for a movie and a softy at Connaught Place in Delhi.

He was a gourmet. With his impeccable taste in clothes and shoes, he made a style statement in his times. Much to my amusement, I was told about his fan following at the marriage of his friend in a village in Sind, Erstwhile Hindustan, or India.

No matter what I reminisce about my father, he is undoubted, the best supporter I ever had in my life. There are many lessons he gave in concise form by turning over the leaves of his past. We did connect over our experiences, our predilections, choices of subjects. I too love to read poetry.

He sat sipping his evening tea and asked me what the novel was, 'A Passage to India' about, the book was a prescribed text for postgraduates. I could see him catching the nuances of the story I related to him, about the perplexing situation a guide finds himself in, a native seeking justice against the colonial masters in the court of law. The heat and dust of the foreign land could create a hallucinatory effect or not. No perfunctory mention, but my father was the pillar of strength and support. I define myself in his image … I am my father's daughter. Never could I understand that patriarchy did indeed occur in the outside world. I take sweet pleasure in tearing to smithereens, the ego of a pernicious idiot, the fool holding the flag of patriarchy.

IT'S A THIN LINE

Aeriel Matthews
Greensboro, North Carolina

In the beginning, when I became aware of my heaven and earth, my dad was a major part of both. As a kid, he was my hero, my wrestling partner, fishing mate, and cheerleader during my county-sponsored basketball games in the third grade. He was a large man. His belly reminded me of a larger version of the barrel that kept my monkeys safe! I used to fall asleep on it as a pillow under his rhythmic breathing while he watched football. He was a tall man with big heavy feet that slid to the kitchen in the middle of the night, eating up my school snacks. I used to get jealous when the neighborhood boys would come by looking for him, as he was the only father figure consistently available in their reach. I was proud to have him as my dad. He held his position as protector of the home, wife, and then two girls as a high priority.

Things slowly began to change with him; he wasn't as joyous as he used to be. While he still loved to protect us, the only thing he didn't protect us from was him. Dad became increasingly violent from fourth grade until I had graduated from college. He embraced being angry and bitter, and I never knew why. He hated when mom would provide her input as it was signed, that she confused his monologues of frustration as dialogue. Yelling and sarcasm would slide through the cracks of my room at one in the morning and alert me to referee the possible fight that may happen. Once I was in his view with panic fueling me to go in front of my mother to protect her, he'd get even angrier and march off to the bedroom. No matter how enraged he became, he never hit my mother, and she never feared, partially her aim was perfect, and she never hesitated to remind him of it.

After some time of growing up in the home with the new, enraged version of my dad, I became just as bitter as him. Begging my mother to leave him in pursuit of a more peaceful and happy life. He would watch my sister and me clean to ensure we hadn't cut corners anywhere, all the while falsely accusing us of disrespectful behavior, sometimes. There was so much pressure to satisfy his need for a perfect family, my mother, sister, and I hated to go home. We stayed out with friends, kept busy with after-school and church in hopes of the next day coming to save us again. He hated having company come by the house and would scold us for the poor quality of friends who come by to see us.

I hate him now. His presence seemed to suffocate the pure joy out of me, and I'd deflate when I'd hear his car pull up. He'd go on to kill some of my joyous occasions, causing trouble at every graduation from middle and high school and even college. But what else could I expect? I'd have to call grandma to come down and talk with him about scarring the family as a child, and now, I've grown to accept his tantrums and still have no idea why he was so angry. Growing up in the church, I began to think he had demons, and I still think that was the case, along with untreated mental illnesses. I know he didn't want to be that person, though, because it would strongly conflict with his loving side. It was literally like living with Dr. Jekyll and Mr. Hyde, which ironically was one of my favorite stories. The sad part is, it'd have to stay that way because he was easily offended and sensitive to the point where if we didn't admit to something that never happened, it was the threat of an unnecessary beating for us two girls at the time and endless arguing with my mother. So, the possibility of having him checked out mentally was out of the plan, to say the least.

It wasn't until I was older, a naïve 20 something year old, to where dad began to calm down, and that was because of his fear of his renal failure, which he refused treatment for, that I began to understand his anger. The disappointment of achieving what he thought was manhood was one log that helped to build the fire. The failure to have the full respect of his wife and children as a provider and father would consume him. We were annoyed with him, afraid of him, and frustrated with lies of paying bills he didn't have the money to pay for; he wanted the respect of someone who earned it, and while he did earn some, he knew we were just putting up with his existence.

He was a man who didn't have anything when he met my mother, who was established. She had her own hair salon out of her home, on her land. When he came along, he couldn't add to her what he didn't have, and this fight for masculinity between a man searching for validity and his independent wife was a large part of the anger he had towards her, which helped me to be bitter and angry towards him. Living over three hours away became a haven for myself, and I'd whisper a bag of prayers to God on behalf of the safety and sanity of my family.

It wasn't until the doctor gave his life expectancy that wouldn't exceed the remainder of the year that I realized we need family therapy to clear all of this up before he dies. After he refused, I left it alone. Towards the end of his life, he seemed to become the man I first met and fell in love with; soft, easy, and approachable. I knew this wasn't necessarily because he was dying. It was the reemerging of who he was. There was no need for anger anymore, it had run its course until there was nothing, but three days left, and for those three days, I got my daddy back.

Throughout our lives together, we had some good moments, although they seem few compared to the bad, we had them. I spent most of my time with him, avoiding him, which was difficult to do in the same house. We didn't get along, but I remained as peaceful as possible to avoid any unhinged wrath. Now, five years after his death, when I speak about him, it's usually in terms of how chaotic, violent, and damaged he was as a person. I hadn't realized how shell-shocked I was from living with him. It was hard to call the verbal assaults, uneasiness when the steps of his feet hit the step to our home abuse. I hadn't seen it as such, and that alone was shocking. Remembering feeling uneasy when trying to go to sleep after he'd gone raving earlier in the night as a child because I was afraid, he'd shoot us all. It was stressful, and the entire time, I knew that wasn't who he was.

When I think about him, I find myself battling, reluctant to call him an abuser, and admitting my love and grief over him to come to light. When talking about it, seeing the faces of my friends used to upset me because I felt they were overreacting. In those moments, I had to reconcile that pulling out a gun on your family is abusive, although again, my mother was strong and unmoved by him. She seemed to have everything in control and would simply tell him to "go on somewhere". I based reality on our reaction to him instead of the truth, because hey, we didn't react like typical victims. I will admit that his effect on me has taught me how to rely on faith and my delusion to get through the moment.

He taught me how to fight as a kid to win petty girl fights in elementary school. We bonded over the one bad hairdo when my mom forgot to do it the night before a basketball game when I was 8. After a few cold globs of pink hair moisturizer, snaps of rubber bands, and hairbows, I laughed when I looked in the mirror but loved it because he did it. I took pictures that day with a proud smile that my daddy did my hair. Outside of survival tactics I learned because of his tyranny, that's what I take away from our time together. Yet, even now, it feels weird to admit my absolute love for him because I know who he wanted to be, and that's not who he was. I must admit, I loved and continually love him. I've resolved that I always will, not because of who he chose to be, but because of the man he felt he never could be.

UNDYING LOVE

Lea Vida Reyes Del Moro
Philippines

"Parents act so strong for us, that we often forget just how fragile they are" Curiano Quotes life

My family lived in a dilapidated wooden house in the simple barrio, and we were lucky to have survived. I was my mother's miracle premature baby, born seven months after a miscarriage and a near death experience. My mother already had five children and as the youngest, weakest, sick child in my family, I had to be protected by my parents. My siblings teased me about my condition.

Despite being poor, we were happy. We still ate three times a day; we went to school and finished our elementary grades with honors. However, my mother kept a secret from us and later died from a heart attack.

Things drastically changed in the months following our mother's death. It forced us to leave our home in the barrio to Manila. My father took care of us despite also being in poor health. He was now our sole provider and seeing him struggle only frustrated us.

My siblings tried their best to help him. They worked in the markets selling fish while attending school. They did other odd jobs by working in fast-food restaurants. As I got older, it was my turn to work; But as I was about to start my job at a fast-food restaurant, my father stepped in. He did his best for us not to lose our schooling. He said that "education was a treasure that no one can take from us."

We performed well in school, received scholarships, and made it to college. We received support from our friends and teachers to earn money for a living. Although our father worked in the market, selling fish and meat and other things, he still could not make enough to cover our expenses.

My siblings moved on and lived their separate lives with their families, but I never left my father. We moved into our house in Manila. He was every part of my life. He was there when I gave birth to my firstborn. For the first time in my life, I felt an unexplainable joy as I saw the brightness shining in my innocent-looking baby's eyes. It was fascinating, and her beauty enchanted me. My heart sank a little, and my hopes and dreams finally came true. I picture out the portrait of a completely happy and loving family and I want to cherish those moments for as I live.

There were several times when my siblings visited our father and brought some of their favorite things from home, including some memorabilia of our childhood memories. While sorting through a mountain of family photos and keepsakes, we laughed at the things father had kept, which included mother old photos and their wedding pictures. We grew up surrounded by photoshoots and pictures. I thought our happiness would never end until later when our father's health deteriorated further and they transferred him to a hospital; They diagnosed him with lung cancer, with only hours to live. He told me to call my siblings for a reunion because he missed my mother and my siblings.

As we gathered around with him, he requested to hold my firstborn's hands. My father's eyes lit up as he stared at the innocent black round eyes of my baby. He wanted to feel the same happiness he felt when he held me in his arms, the cry of a sleeping baby, the fear of my childhood. I think my father, without really admitting it, felt that the love that was lost over the years had filled her again through my firstborn child. I couldn't help it, but tears were rushing from my eyes.

My second sister, Lisa, recorded while father told us how much he loved us through the years, and he sang a lullaby song to make the baby fall asleep. It was so heartbreaking as our lives tore apart, witnessing the agony of my father writhing and suffering from pain, recalling our years living in poverty.

My heart tried to reject the pain, and it pulled me into a blackness that cut out whole seconds or maybe even forever the agony, making it that much harder to keep us with reality. We lost our father, and we will never see him again, just like our mother, but his memories and love remain in our hearts and soul forever. My father passed away, surrounded by his children and his siblings. We quietly listened to the recordings of where my firstborn child gave him so much joy.

"Parents act so strongly for us we often forget just how fragile they are." They endure pain and sacrifice almost their whole lives just to give the needs of their children. The sacrifices our parents made for their children will affect us when we become parents, too. I've made the same sacrifices for my baby, like how my mother and father treated me. My parents became the ultimate heroes that defend their children, and they never gave up, instilling the importance of education.

I will cherish the memories my father left us. Our last reunion as a family marked a glorious moment in our family as we remembered the old times when we lived a simple, poor life.

LET'S MEET AGAIN

Shatara S. Clark
Montgomery, Alabama

A few years ago, I wrote a blog post on Father's Day addressed to the girl who feels fatherless on Father's Day. I related so well to that girl, I felt that girl's pain, and I wanted her to know that she was not alone. Ironically my father had a huge hand in raising me and had been in my life since the day that I was born so my story is not very typical, but it is painful, and it is real.

They told me that as a baby my dad had to sneak out of the back door to avoid waking me up after HE had to put me to sleep because I was not friendly to anybody else, and I would not allow him to leave me. I adored him and I always wanted him around. When he and my mom would fight (viciously) I would cry so bad because I never wanted them to divorce, and I never wanted my dad to have to leave me. As I got older though, I started to understand the fights: dad was an adulterer and an alcoholic. Sadly, around the tender age of about 10, I finally saw this firsthand.

We lived in a small community and people "talked." Children would come to school and report to me that they saw my dad with other women, that they saw my dad drunk, that my dad tried drugs, and so much more. Pretty embarrassing right? Kids are cruel so of course; they didn't whisper when they made the morning announcements. From there I became very aware and most of my innocence and googly eyes for my dad was diminishing. Soon after, around the age of 13, I walked into a store and a girl from a neighboring middle school told me she didn't know that I had a sister. I replied, "yea I have two older sisters." She went on to explain that I indeed had a younger sister (one year younger to be exact) that went to her school. I remember fuming and becoming so embarrassed at the fact that I had no idea what she was talking about that I just exited the store. I asked my mom about it, and she brushed it off as rumors. As soon as I could I asked my dad and he just said it was a "grown folks' story." I was so angry for so many reasons: I had no idea who this girl was, it was obvious that dad had been unfaithful, and no one wanted to give me answers. Once I entered high school I demanded to know more, so dad began to take me to visit her, and we tried to form a friendship until she moved away.

After high school, dad's drinking continued, and it was just awful. He would come in complaining and I would try to push myself to sleep so I could miss him and the argument that was likely to follow. It was not a happy time for me. He wouldn't maintain employment, money was tight, and it was just something all the time. Teenage years were just painful and stressful. I was an outgoing person so always having to hear that we couldn't afford things broke my spirit and I began to resent my dad for not being the provider that I felt God had called him to be. By the grace of God, I made it through high school, and I never lacked, and I entered college and graduated on time. It felt good to be out of that house and only having to visit and even then, I didn't have to stay long. I hated leaving my mom there, but that was her husband.

After graduating from college, I eventually moved to a different city with my fiancé. As we began planning our wedding, my dad began acting strangely at home. He was staying away a whole lot claiming he was working. He wasn't accepting help from my mom in preparation for my wedding or anything. It was just strange. Then one day my mom called and stated that my dad had moved out! I was baffled because they had been together for over 25 years so I could not understand what caused this. When I spoke with my dad, he claimed they were just having issues and he had to leave, and he was living in an apartment.

I tried to accept what my dad told me, but my intuition told me he was lying. Soon my mom confirmed it: She called my mom to alert her that my dad would be living with her now. I was in shock. Sure, my dad had a wandering eye and did many terrible things, but I never thought that my dad would leave. This was unreal and so disappointing especially with my nuptials right around the corner. Little did I know the ultimate portrayal was to come.

I was sitting with my fiancé watching one of our favorite shows at the time (True Blood) when I received a text message with a link. I opened it to find that my father had married this woman while STILL being married to my mother! I was no longer shocked, I was pissed! This was beyond disrespectful and at this point, it left no regard for my mother. I immediately wrote my father off, banned him from my wedding, and moved on with my planning and life. At that point, it didn't matter to me if I ever heard from him again.

Years passed and so many harsh words came and went, looks that could kill, and so much more. Hate was in my heart for him and her; the woman who destroyed the pieced-together family that I had. Six years later, I received a call from my younger sister (dads' daughter). She had come to terms with everything and wanted to get to know dad and that side of the family. I respected her decision, but at the time I was in an even more bitter place, and I was not about to go around "those people." I was proud of her for her decision though.

About two years after that which places us now at eight years, I finally begin to have decent conversations with my father that kind of just sprung up from me becoming tired of hating him. I want to believe that the death of my grandmother (his mother) who was a pure angel on earth had a ton to do with my change of heart. I knew that life is short, and I also knew that to enter heaven I couldn't continue harboring unforgiveness. Those conversations led to my sister and I talking again and her planning another visit here. This time we all decided to get together.

COVID-19 came close to stopping our reunion, but it did not. The three of us came together that day and fellowshipped and mended. I had to understand that as humans we are the product of our parents, and environments, and although our parents do the best that they can with us, DNA is a whole other thing, generational curses are a whole other thing in addition to lineage and sometimes our actions which are terrible to others are the right thing for us. I am sure my father knows that he went about things in the very wrong manner, but whether he knows or not, I know what God loves and that is forgiveness. I have also forgiven his new wife and we are slowly getting to know each other. I am not angry with either of them anymore and it's so much easier, and healthier. My father and I had to meet again, just as we did on the day that I was born. A clean slate is ours.

DAD'S YIDDISH LETTERS

Lois Perch Villemaire
Annapolis, Maryland

Dad was a collector of things, especially antiques and unusual treasures with a good story. He would attend auctions and purchase smelly old steamer trunks filled with miscellaneous items. The excitement was unpacking them at home. He let us help. Dad had a collection of old clocks that sounded on the quarter-hour, antiquated typewriters that no longer functioned, and oversized volumes of newspapers published during the Civil War. He joined the Danbury Mint and received a classic car model with an ownership certificate each month, creating a vast collection. For a while, he was an avid stamp collector, and we followed suit with our beginner albums and packets of hinges.

His favorite piece was a glorious vintage music box. He transported it home from the auction in two sections - a fancy-footed, carved oak cabinet filled with musical metal discs and the matching music box placed on top. The ornate antique stood about four feet high. When it played, the clear tones were louder than expected, reverberating around the living room like xylophones and bells. Dad had a passion for old magazines, newspapers, and books. He liked to collect artwork, sculptures, and pottery. Mom wasn't involved in the acquisition process, but she enjoyed decorating the house with unique conversation pieces.

There were other ways that I felt his influence. His love of music, food, sports, and entertainment was infectious. We may have been the only kids who knew the words to every song in the movie, The Jolson Story (released in 1946), as well as most of the film's dialogue. As one of his favorites, we viewed it many times. Dad wasn't perfect. He had mood swings, and we were quick to observe and determine if he was in a bad mood. Sometimes a bad mood was associated with a headache. He didn't like to socialize, so if Mom scheduled an event that she wanted him to attend, she waited until the last minute to tell him about it. That way, she reasoned, he didn't have much time to complain. Mom was the disciplinarian, and Dad was the fun person. He took us bowling, to baseball games, and out to lunch at his favorite places.

Not long after he passed away in 2016, I became inspired by the enthusiasm he had demonstrated for genealogy. Armed with some of the information he had accumulated, I began to dabble in family research. Dad didn't have the opportunity to enjoy the convenient methods of searching online for family history. He would have loved it.

One day while going through a large plastic tub of family photos and documents, I came across an envelope marked "Letters to Zayda 1944-1945." I discovered nine letters in perfect condition written in what I recognized as Yiddish. I couldn't read or understand a word of it, but from the label on the envelope, it was clear that Dad had written the letters long ago to his grandparents.

What a gift I had been given! It was Dad's 23-year-old voice in letters he wrote over 75 years ago during World War II. He reported for basic training in April 1944 at Keesler Field in Mississippi, quite a distance from his hometown of Philadelphia, where he lived with his parents and younger sister. He was very close with his grandparents. From previous marriages, his grandmother (Fannie) had a daughter, and his grandfather (Louis) had a son, along with other siblings. They created a blended family when they married in 1914. To tie the family together, like a nice, neat package, Fannie's daughter, Rose, and Louis' older son, Morris, married on New Year's Eve in 1919. Since the father of his father was married to the mother of his mother, Dad grew up with one set of grandparents.

The extended family lived together during his childhood years. Yiddish was spoken in the home. Later, they lived apart but in the same neighborhood. Dad was the oldest grandchild and had a special relationship with his grandfather, he was called Zayda.

After checking for recommendations, I overnighted the precious letters to a Yiddish translator in Chicago. She explained we would achieve better results if she worked from the originals. She calculated the rate based on estimating the time required for this project.

"Please include a check in the package," she said.

It took no time at all, maybe 24 hours after receipt, for an email to arrive with the full translations, and she assured me that she would return the originals by mail. What did I discover about Dad in those letters? I kept in mind that he was a 23-year-old "city boy" who had lived at home and was beginning basic training in the army in Mississippi during the war. Quite an adjustment.

In the letters, Dad was very careful to reassure his grandparents that he was happy and getting along well in his new "job" as a soldier. He was thrilled to be able to write to them in their familiar Yiddish and loved receiving their letters. He said that his Jewish friends envied those communications.

He cared about his grandparents and worried about their health. At that time, they were ages 66 and 73, and I'm sure that seemed old to young Dad. He asked about his grandfather's bad stomach and suggested that they both stay indoors on very hot days.

He offered some information about his daily life in basic training. He reflected on the monotony of eating, drinking, working, marching in rows, and sleeping but presented his routine in an upbeat way. He was pleased with the way he looked in his uniform.

Dad must have had a run-in at first with the drill sergeant, who he called "a dog," but later reported that the relationship improved. Days went by quickly. He enjoyed his work and looked forward to weekends when he could sleep late and go to the movies or play cards. He asked them to write as often as possible and promised to call but explained that phone calls had to be brief due to the long line at the payphones.

There was an issue that he shared concerning his teeth. He had visited the Army dentist for a routine appointment. The dentist wanted to extract many of his teeth based on the diagnosis that his teeth were bad, and they would certainly become painful if they weren't already. Dad said his teeth didn't hurt and refused to allow them to be pulled. The dentist reiterated that eventually, they would be a problem. Dad conceded that he would return at that time. He confided in the letter that he was glad to get out of that appointment with all his teeth!

There was an interesting exchange in two of the letters about a girlfriend, Betty. They had broken up, but Dad had decided to write to her. Betty responded negatively, and Dad told his grandparents that she was very unhappy with him. He confided in them that he cared about her, but memories were beginning to fade. I wonder if she expected more from him before he left. An engagement ring, perhaps? We'll never know. I do know that he met Mom when he returned to Philadelphia after completing two years in the service, and they married in 1947.

The messages of years ago were from a kind and caring young man, so much like the dad of five, he would become. He was there for us in good and difficult times and was married to Mom for 65 years until she passed away in 2012. I think he preserved the letters along with family memorabilia to someday be discovered and reread.

I'm glad to be the one to have come across his special words to those he loved.

MOM TAUGHT ME INFORMATION DAD TAUGHT ME TO THINK

Zoe Fawkes
Kansas City, Missouri

I was home-schooled from K-12, much to the curiosity of everyone around us, who could not fathom an education that took place outside of a classroom and involved one's parents. I couldn't fathom one where I had to compete with dozens of other students for help and attention and had to learn at the pace of the group. I had no idea the privilege I had to receive my mother's attention, divided only with my sister.

My dad was less accessible in every way, but that made him the prize. Scarcity increases value, and dad was sparse with emotional connection, time, and presence in the home. So, when we caught those moments of leisure time with him, we felt lavished with unearned abundance. And for me, that meant brain Olympics.

It is heart-wrenching to think of it now; the marathon conversations he would put me through, playing devil's advocate, and coaxing me into perspectives I did not know how to articulate. I reacted defensively, like a cornered animal, as he challenged my worldview and made me rethink the history my mother had taught me. She never taught me anything overtly wrong, but it had a strong nationalist flavor and a sprinkling of white supremacy that seasoned all of America's textbooks in the 20th century. If I started questioning those narratives as I reached my teen years, if I started to pick apart the logical fallacies of academics, if I began to squint skeptically at the rows of books on my shelf written only by white, male, American authors, it was because of dad.

He was the one who reminded me, when I spoke defensively of American nuclear power, that the United States was the only country to deploy such a weapon, and of the devastation it caused. He was the one who asked why I wasn't considering moving to another country if I wanted to learn another language so badly. He was the one who dropped hints that marriage was not the only option for women. He was the one who removed us from an abusively conservative organization that was teaching my sister and me that we were the property of the men in our lives. He was the one who watched John Wayne movies and then talked about violent colonialism and toxic masculinity. He never used those words, but that's what he was doing.

Those conversations don't happen in the same way, now. My deeply philosophical, challenging all assumption father is gone. His agile mind has been eaten away. One might assume I am about to divulge a disease, some degenerative syndrome. I suppose I am, but it's none of the ones you are thinking of.

I lost my father to a narrative of victimization that he found too compelling to refute. I lost him to Fox News and the sympathy of white, cishet males for other white, cishet males. I lost him to a simpler narrative in which he was the hero, not the villain.

My father, passive and non-violent by nature, became increasingly authoritarian and avidly defensive of American military action. My father, the thoughtful and deep thinker that he was, became a mouthpiece for over-simplified conservative talking points that brushed snowflake liberalism aside with a sweep of the machine-gun barrel. My father, fair-minded and educated, began to dismiss objective knowledge and expertise, assuming the worst of those unlike himself, and disregarding the opinions of those he thought too "elite."

He has never been comfortable with his status in the world; that much did not change. He disliked that he was elite. He was never comfortable with the fact that he came from wealth and held multiple degrees. He used "howdy," as though anyone from Pasadena had ever non-ironically greeted someone with "howdy." He spoke of anti-science rhetoric compassionately even while he worked in the medical field. He always held his intelligence and power uncomfortably, awkwardly, as though it had been handed to the wrong person; a person who did not know how to wield it. He only became comfortable weaponizing it when he thought he was passing for a yokel. If he played the simple country boy long enough, people would forget about his intelligence, doctorate, huge inheritance…But I never did. I've always known what he was and how that was transferred to me. He hid our wealth from me, to be sure, but I always knew how deep his soul went and how broad his mind reached.

This quite literal embarrassment of riches was easier for him to hide as conservatism became a movement of populism. He could hide the tax benefits received only by the wealthy behind a drawl. He could leverage friendships with manual laborers to justify an anti-union policy. He could preach a simple, unexamined faith to decry the immoral left. He could benefit from all the invisible power he held without anyone calling out his privilege. And that having cake and eating it too was just too appealing. It was too perfect. Who, in their right mind, would persist in challenging corruption, in uplifting the interests of the less fortunate masses, or combating racism, if they never had to be held accountable?

And that is how I lost my father. To the happily-ever-after of fairy-tale white patriarchy. I lost him to female pastors whose authority he could dismiss by quoting scripture. I lost him to pundits who looked and talked like him and who stroked his raised hackles into submission with assurances that he had the right to it. As long as the other side was killing babies and destroying the family, he was promised, he had a claim to moral superiority. And if that claim also led to higher levels of political power and economic gain, so be it. That's just the way the system is. No one's fault. This is your right. Shame others can't have it, too, but that's on them. You deserve this, poor, beleaguered white man.

Maybe he always thought this way, but he enjoyed the sport of debate and loved cornering his intelligent daughter in conversation, forcing her to defend the past answers she gave to every question.

AT PEACE WITH WHAT HE COULD GIVE

Lisa A. Crothers-Vermette
Wells, Maine

A reflective void, wavering peace, the esteem of either positive or negative outcomes, all manifests with the complex-simple relationship, that of father and daughter. The adult product of us, either reveals a lifetime of peace and greater insight into other relationships or propels us on a journey of unanswered questions that fosters a lifelong searching for responses that may never give us a satisfactory understanding. So, it is this basic human relationship, the acceptance of what the person can give and not what they are expected to give, which opens our lives to others and a heart either filled with contentment or an emotional roller coaster of anger and anxiety.

As with many of my peers in the 80s, divorce was as normal as getting up and going to school and so, young sons and daughters were impacted in both positive and negative ways, some still struggling today. For me, the idea of two separate homes was a welcome respite from the constant one-sided screaming of an unhappy marriage with no end in sight. But there came the waiting. It was the waiting ...and waiting and constant waiting for the harmonious two-separate homes to arrive bringing us all a bit of relief. For me, the peace I craved in that two-separate home scenario from the screaming, blaming, unhappy individual cast as my mother never came. That was 1977. I was 8.

In 1977, Jimmy Carter was sworn in as president and Fleetwood Mac's Rumors hit the charts. Perhaps though the greatest single event of 1977, other than my parent's divorce, was the beginning of the Star Wars legacy. Everyone in school had already been to the theater, experiencing this cultural explosion and the excitement continued to build. My younger brother and I could not wait to be part of the conversation about this energetic phenomenon. So much was happening in the world, yet so little in our lives seemed to push forward. We moved into a small apartment with our maternal grandparents, six aunts, and uncles, and a baby cousin. Scheduled to see my dad every Wednesday, only a handful of short visits spanning several months or so actually occurred.

Finally, word arrived! Dad was going to pick us up on Wednesday and we were going to see *Star Wars* at the Charles Theater in Boston. My heart skipped a beat, I told everyone at school. Finally, Wednesday arrived, and my brother and I waited on the outside stoop of the apartment building. We waited and waited. With anger and clenched fists, my brother cried and went inside. Long after the movie started, I waited. He never came. I didn't want to go to school Thursday morning, but with the screeching of my mother's voice, "I told you so! I told you he wouldn't show up!" I knew I was better off at school under the poking of my classmates for my dad is what I excused as "sick" that Wednesday night and missing the movie, then at home under the berating hatred of my mother.

The same routine followed Wednesday after Wednesday. Stoop. No-show. Stoop. No-show. Like a sore wound, my mother could not contain herself and continued to offer bitter words and a sour disposition. "See, I told you don't bother to sit outside and wait for him." Eventually, we did see Star Wars. He showed up one faith-filled sunny Wednesday afternoon. Taking the bus into town we walked several blocks to the theater and settled into seats with candy, popcorn, and soda. It was a grand night. No excuses were offered for missed Wednesdays, only laughing, and joking. By then, however, I knew it best to always stay alert, it was safer than the disappointment of an emotional letdown of a no-show my friends of divorced families shared, and so, I was content in the time he gave and in the present moments lived.

By the time I was 10, dad was happily remarried with a new family, stepdaughter included. Random visits included the stepmother's good womanly advice to lady friends on the phone, my dad watching TV, and a stepsister who smoked and dated boys. My brother never came, by then he had given up. In a couple of years, he moved to another State, married wife number three, and I did not hear from him for quite a long time. When that call finally came shortly before Christmas my anticipation once again ignited. The magical voice and excitement of your dad! I believed him, every word he said, but when the

Christmas presents arrived long after the new year, there were no records or paints, no books or jewelry in that brown cardboard package. No Christmas cards, wrapping paper, or chocolates. A haphazard box filled with random adult-sized T-shirts, of no particular significance or meaning, in sizes not fitting of young children, sat near the trash barrel.

With the magical evening of Star Wars long past, the sporadic calls faded away after the arrival of a hodgepodge of leftover tee-shirts. I never cried or harbored anger as the counterbalance of my mother's berating and screeching gave a subconscious understanding and perhaps innate sympathy became the autonomic response for a lost soul, the soul of my father. He was a laid-back, good-natured, humorous person with a contented disposition, just as the rhythmic floating in-and-out of people's lives – mine, my brother's, his parent's, and my mother's. A soul perhaps devoured by immigrant parents in a foreign country stripped of their Polish heritage, a political war in a foreign land, and a wife filled with hatred for the entire world wearing a robe of narcissism. And so, it went on like this, my dad floated into and then once again out of my life until I was married and a parent myself.

"Your focus determines your reality." Insightful words of Qui-Gon Jinn (*Star Wars Episode I: The Phantom Menace*). In reflecting on the marks his behavior left on me, as a daughter, as a parent, as a friend, the relationship itself was rhythmic and cyclical. I did not focus on a relationship of disappointment due to the constant flowing in and out of my life. The short periods of involvement were overcast by long periods of absence and silence. He missed my wedding and the birth of all four of my children, not knowing them until his youngest grandson was well into his toddlerhood. I learned to take it in stride and to be settled and at peace with the "normal" of our relationship, understanding that perhaps that is all he could give any one person.

We are now in that receding space once again, I believe, however, for the final time as he floats out of this life for good. He has in recent years remarried my mother, despite all the advice given him regarding her unchanged nature of narcissism and badge of unhappiness, yet despite it all, his unobtrusive, good-natured humor still resides. For myself, I have learned the importance of commitment and keeping your word, to be sensitive in disappointing people, because we will, most often, unknowingly. The critical factor for me is not allowing a lifetime of floating in and out of my life to determine my focus, allowing it to take control, fostering anger, and using it to place blame and dictate my reality.

It is this last retreat, this last moment he will not show, I glean my greatest insight, the moment of unconditional love and acceptance of all he was able to give. As the culprit of dementia takes over my dad, he retreats into an unsettled world, yet a place he was confident and secure, a place where he was in charge and control, in the war-torn jungles of Vietnam. It is in this final retreat of his daughter, of his life, I gain the most, a moment where I have clarity of who he is and why I am this way today.

I was born on the day he arrived home from his final tour in Vietnam. I didn't understand the impact of this significant occasion and the regret he lived with not signing on for a third tour. "I wanted to go back, but well, you know how it is sometimes." As I listen to the stories of his distant life, they are not ones filled with that of children, grandchildren, or a full childhood, stories of holidays and recipes of practical jokes and family vacations. I listen to stories of patriotism, brotherhood, heroism, and loss, even regret. His walls are covered with memorabilia from two tours in Vietnam as part of the 101ˢᵗ Engineering Battalion, a snapshot in time he never resolved, never came to terms with, never left in the past. There are no photo books of a life filled with his journey, only artifacts in remembrance of a moment in time, in his personal history.

I think of the years, of his presence and disappearance, and how every time we reconnected, it truly was a happy moment. They were not filled with resentment or anger, questions of *why have you abandoned me again, where have you been all this time, what did I do wrong*. His nature was not that of arrogance but an inward reflection. I know people, my peers, still struggling with anxiety linked to this type of "abandonment." They are truly fraught, and I am sad for them, grieving silently, sitting in no judgment, wishing for them the peace I know.

In my own life, the relationship with my father is reflected in the long-term friendships I have nurtured over the years. In thinking about my 4 best girl pals, the longest being over 40 years and the shortest 15. I look at the ebb and flow of each of the relationships, recognizing that there were long periods when we were not as connected in our daily routines and life's rituals, yet the moments of reconnecting were always a simple picking up where we left off, not missing a beat. This is what I have gained from that relationship with my father. There was a possibility of true feelings of abandonment, exasperating into anxiety and the distrusting of people and a likelihood of poor relationships along my path, but I simply chose differently.

It is easy to fall into despair and blame. Relationships are hard and take active work but in essence, it is all in the way you approach it. I am at peace with the ebb and flow of the relationship with my father and look not at what he could not give me, but at what he went through in a historical moment in his life and what he gave me along his journey. I miss who he was as dementia progresses, but I am grateful for the moments he flowed into and out of my life. I am at peace with all he could give and not my expectations of what it should have be

THE MILK CARTON

Melissa Siig
Tahoe City, California

I scanned the arrival area at Ben Gurion Airport in Tel Aviv for my father, pulling my suitcase behind me. He was normally always there in the crowd, jumping up and down, waving his arms up in the air, and shouting "Melissa!" in his Israeli accent. I pictured him in his 40s and 50s, wearing khaki pants with a nice button-down shirt tucked into his pants. He would have a big smile on his face, and when he finally saw me, he would give me a big hug and say, "Melissa, you made it!" And he would take my suitcase from me and lead me to the car.

So, I was not prepared for what I saw. I couldn't find him at first. It was an odd feeling for a moment to think that maybe my father had forgotten to pick us up or decided not to come. But then he was in front of me. His front tooth was chipped, he wore dirty cargo shorts and an old, stained t-shirt, and his face was drawn and saggy. He looked like a homeless person. I stifled a gasp while at the same time my heart broke a little more. I wanted to look away, to run away, but I was here to see him.

"Melissa, there you are!" he said, seemingly unaware of the impact his appearance had on me, or maybe unaware of his appearance entirely. He held up his hand for a type of high-five and then hugged me.

"You made it. Where are the others?"

I watched as my three kids walked up and said, "Hi *Saba*," the Hebrew word for grandfather. They awkwardly embraced him, this man they hardly knew.

"You are all here! Good to see you. How was the flight? Where is Anna?"

My sister Anna and her husband, Jeff, and three-year-old son, Avi, were right behind us. Anna had rented a car and agreed to take one of my kids with them so the rest of us would fit in my dad's car. I looked on with envy as Anna and Jeff walked away with my daughter Kaya in tow towards the rental car desk. Anna waved to me with a sly smile that I interpreted as "Good luck, sucker."

"OK, let's go get the car, if I can remember where it is," my dad said. "When was the last time you were here? Nine years ago, right? I still have the same car!"

The car was a 1991 navy blue Volvo sedan that he had been driving since my grandfather passed away in 1998. It had been my grandfather's car, and I'm sure my father was trying to hold onto a piece of his father. Or maybe he was just too frugal to buy a new car. When we squeezed inside, I was horrified to realize the Volvo was in the same shape as my dad – torn and grimy fabric hung down like a curtain from what had once been the car's ceiling, and I had to lift it behind my head to see out the front window. The seats were ripped. The inside of the car doors had holes in them. Kaiden tried to roll down the window by looking for a button to push until I finally instructed him to roll it down the old-fashioned way, with the handle. Everywhere I looked there were holes and tears and stains. The car was grubby and outdated and badly in need of repairs, much like my father.

I made Siig sit in the front with my dad because I didn't think I could handle it. And then, being the good Jewish girl that I was, I made the sign of the cross in front of my heart. I had forgotten that my dad's driving skills had deteriorated over the last few years, and I kicked myself for living in the past, for only remembering my dad as he was in middle age. Now he was in his early 70s, and he was about to drive in a city that was not his own. In rush hour.

I had hoped that Siig, who was a master at Google Maps and Waze, could help navigate my father through the busy freeways and streets of Tel Aviv to the Airbnb we had rented on Rothschild Boulevard in the heart of Tel Aviv. But I should have known better.

We exited the airport through a maze of perimeters, barriers, and armed soldiers. The airport, much like Israel itself, had greatly expanded and changed since I was a girl. We got on Highway 1, which was clogged with cars, and slowly made our way toward the high rises and skyscrapers of Tel Aviv. I cracked a window open, letting the salty Mediterranean air waft in, momentarily covering up the stale smell of the car.

"Yedu, Google Maps says if we take this exit, we can avoid some traffic and get to the apartment," Siig said.

"What? No, no, no. You take exit 10 to get to Dizengoff. That's how it's always done," he said as he drove past the exit.

It was obvious that my father had no idea how Google Maps worked. He had used a film camera until he finally got an iPad a few years ago. When my kids were little, after my father would take a photo of them, they would run up to him yelling, "We want to see! We want to see!" And then when my dad curiously handed them his camera, they would look on the back and make swiping motions to no avail, and then give it back to him, confused and no longer interested.

Things got more precarious once we got off the highway. My dad came within inches of hitting other cars on several occasions, breaking just in the nick of time. I could feel my shoulders inching up toward my ears, tension building in my neck. I gripped the front seat, cursing myself for putting my family in jeopardy. Every time there was a near miss, I let out an involuntary "Jesus Christ." Siig turned around and gave me a stern look, "You are not helping things, Melissa."

My dad stopped in front of an electronics store in a run-down building.

"This is where the apartment is. This should be number 14 since across the street is 15."

"Yuda, this is an odd-numbered block. We need to go one more block to get to the even numbers," Siig told him.

"No, no, no. This is where it should be."

Siig turned around in the front seat and gave me a hard look. My dad was not getting it. Finally, when we saw the sign for a parking lot, Siig convinced him it was best to park there and then find the apartment.I vowed that I would not get into the car again for our entire five days in Tel Aviv.

Months later, my dad called on Kaya's 13th birthday. I nonchalantly asked him what year the Volvo was. "Why do you want it?" he asked.

"No, I was just telling someone about the car and wanted to know what year it was," I lied.
And then he dropped a bombshell on me.

"I still owe you for the Mustang so maybe I'll give you the Volvo," he joked.

My jaw dropped. Motherfucker. So, he wasn't oblivious after all. He had always promised me when I was young that his 1973 convertible Mustang would be mine when I turned 16, then sold it with no compunction before he moved back to Israel a few years before I was to get my driver's license

In Tel Aviv, my dad was difficult to talk with. He hovered over his iPad most of the time, doing whatever he did there, reading the news and checking prices of commodities and stocks, scribbling notes on the small piece of paper he always kept in his pocket. Talking with him sometimes felt futile, like he was only half-listening and presumed he knew the answers. It was ironic that he had become like his mother, my *Safta*, who was notorious for her endless talking and telling stories that went on forever. When she was alive, my father could only take so much and usually interrupted her with, *"Eima, shekit, die!" (Mother, shut up, enough!)* And now, my father was repeating the sins of his mother. A simple question about Jerusalem exacted a 30-minute historical foray into the battle between the Palestinians and Israelis over the city. It didn't matter if anybody was listening.

I would try to bond with him over topics where we could converse: Israeli or American politics, updates on family members. But my dad would usually hijack the conversation.

"So, Melissa, what do you think of Trump and immigration?" he asked one afternoon as he sat at the dining room table tearing off pieces of pita bread and dipping it into hummus. I wondered if he would offer to buy groceries at all during our five days in Tel Aviv. "He is a lot like Netanyahu, you know."

"I don't agree with his policies at all. The immigrants are just people seeking a better life, they…"

"No, no," he interrupted me. "Can you imagine if Trump let every single person in? He has to protect the borders."

I tuned him out, knowing I would not be able to make my point. It was sometimes easier to agree with him or let him drone on, otherwise, it was too much effort to state my side.

One day my cousins, two sisters, Maya and Tom, came to visit with Tom's two-year-old daughter in tow, who twisted and cried in her arms. Tom, who also had a four-year-old daughter and was a full-time lawyer, seemed exasperated.

"It's hard," she told us.

This elicited a lecture from my father about the difficulty of raising girls. My eyes bulged at this comment. Did he raise us? He left when I was 14, Julie was 11, and Anna was two. Since then, he had been completely disengaged. That's why my mother had been upset when I had asked my dad to walk me down the aisle at my wedding. "I raised you, not him," she said. But I felt guilty.

The thing was, I loved him. He was a good person inside, and I knew he loved us, he had just made a series of bad, selfish choices since the divorce that seemed to compound one another. As my mom said, "Daddy walks around with blinders on." I am sure he was suffering somewhere deep inside from his decisions.

But then he would do things that surprised me, like paying for dinner one night or buying groceries with Anna, although Anna told me he tried to argue her out of almost every item. "Anna, why do you need two things of cottage cheese?"

One day in the apartment in Tel Aviv, he came home exhausted from an outing with Anna and her family to Jerusalem. He tumbled into his bed and quickly fell asleep. He wasn't used to sightseeing, especially with a toddler. I walked downstairs to check on him and saw his semi-bald head of dyed-black hair, like the outline of where a *yarmulke* should be, resting on the pillow. I hovered over him, staring, as a mother might gaze at her sleeping child. I had the urge to lie next to him and wrap my arms around him. He had been a good father before he left. Where had he gone so wrong?

The next morning, I had to get out of the house. I went to the corner market to buy more milk, but instead of going straight back to the apartment, I found myself turning right on the wide pedestrian promenade in the middle of Rothschild Boulevard shaded by ficus trees, the carton of milk sweating in the plastic bag. Tears streamed down my face as I kept walking, passing espresso kiosks and mini-parks and people walking their dogs. I passed a couple of salsa dancing and families picnicking on blankets. I stared up at the white Bauhaus buildings from the 1920s that lined the boulevard, many filled with trendy restaurants. I walked until I reached the end. Then I wiped my eyes under my sunglasses and turned around. Why, I wondered, didn't I feel like this when I was in Israel nine years ago? I hadn't cried at all back then, in fact, I had enjoyed my trip, but now I couldn't stop crying.

I had come to Israel to be with my dad, but instead, I found myself avoiding him. It was too painful, too difficult. I thought Anna was brave for inviting him along with her to tour Jerusalem. I couldn't imagine spending an entire day with him. It was much easier to go off with Siig and the kids. We rented scooters and bikes, checked out the old city of Jaffa, went to the beach, swam in the warm Mediterranean while avoiding jellyfish, and visited the Tel Aviv Museum where Maya is a curator. Almost nothing with my father.

I had come to Israel to be with my dad, but this shell of a man was not my father. He was something else, hollow, and stubborn and self-centered. The dad of my childhood was gone.

When I got back to the apartment and opened the fridge, there was already a fresh carton of milk inside. "Julie and I went and bought milk," my dad told me. "Where have you been?"

MY FATHER, MY HERO

Tara Conrad
Scranton, Pennsylvania

My best friend. My first love. My hero. All words that describe my Daddy. I realize how fortunate I have been to have a father who was present and active. Looking through our family photo albums our story unfolds. A two-year-old me standing inside my dad's military boots. Four-year-old me, having her saddle shoes tied by dad on my first day of kindergarten. Ten-year-old me climbing trees and hanging upside down with dad doing the same next to me. He is a part of all my favorite memories.

My dad is a veteran. He volunteered to serve his country in Vietnam. As part of the Army's First Cavalry Division, he was a machine gunner in a helicopter. Our local airport used to have an airshow every year. By some odd chance, the actual helicopter he flew in Vietnam was there one year. Few daughters can say they sat in the very spot their father did while he was defending his country, but I can. It was an honor that, even now, sends shivers down my spine.

A sobering memory regarding his service never fails to overcome me with emotion. The Moving Wall, the traveling memorial to Vietnam Veterans who lost their lives, made a local stop years ago. Dad wanted to go. He wanted to pay respect to fellow soldiers, friends lost in battle. It was a hot day. People were milling about, but there was no sound. Even the birds were silent in their reverence. I stood back and watched as my father searched and located the men's names. As I watched him search, a story he once told me played in my head. My father, then still a young man, had been up flying long past the number of hours *allowed*. He landed, only to have to go right back up. A man, a fellow soldier, and a friend of my father's told him to go get some sleep, that he would take this mission for him. Unknown to the soldier, that mission would be his last. The helicopter was shot down—no survivors. I don't know the man's name, but he gave his life in place of my dad's. Words aren't enough to express gratitude for his selfless actions. Without them, I wouldn't be here today.

My father has always been an avid outdoorsman. He loved the outdoors and wanted to share his passion for it with me. Although I didn't share his love for hunting, I loved going out into nature. We went on many adventures hiking through the forests of northeastern Pennsylvania. Dad showed me what berries were safe to eat, ones I lovingly nicknamed "Bear Berries." He taught me how to walk quietly, something I wasn't very good at, so I didn't scare the wildlife around us. One of my favorite memories is from the day we were out, and I was sitting by a railroad bed looking for lizards hiding beneath the rocks. "Gumpie," Dad used his nickname for me. "If we sit still and quiet you might see an animal." After sitting for what felt like forever, I looked up and saw a fawn no more than five feet away. The fawn looked at me, its eyes holding no fear, rather it mirrored the curiosity that was in mine. I held my breath, not wanting to scare the baby deer as it grazed along the forest's edge. Eventually, the fawn finished eating whatever it had found and turned, walking away slowly. It was a moment in my life I'll never forget. A lesson learned from my father about the beauty found in moments of quiet and patience.

Dad was a talented fisherman who tied his flies to mimic ones found locally. Many nights he spent at his worn wooden desk. The clamp held a tiny hook as he meticulously wrapped strings and feathers creating something beautiful in preparation for the next day's fishing trip. When we arrived at the lake, he slipped into his hip boots and with his fly rod in hand, he would wade into the flowing water. The actions were well-choreographed. His arm lifted, sending the line gracefully floating through the air before it gently skipped across the surface of the water. I would sit mesmerized watching him repeat the action over and over until a fish would bite and he would reel it in. "It's all in the wrist." He would tell me.

I didn't get his talent for fishing either. With my pole in hand, I would hold up my arm, trying my best to mimic his actions. *It's all in the wrist* on repeat in my head. My line would fly, tangling as it went. *Plop.* The hook and bobber collided with the water creating a huge splash and scaring everything around. In my attempts to reel it back in, I would inevitably get it stuck in the rocks and weeds on the bottom of the lake. Dad would set his pole down and patiently come over and fix my mess only to have me repeat it all day long. Thinking back, I laugh at the memories and wonder how he was always so patient with me. I guess that's why he brought those Kit-Kat bars and would tell me to go sit and have a snack.

Some of the most special memories are from my wedding day. It was the first day I had ever seen my dad dressed in a tuxedo. He looked so handsome and proud as he was about to walk his only child down the aisle. I can imagine it wasn't easy to pass my hand and the responsibility of loving and caring for me, to the young man I was about to marry, yet he did it with such grace. The realization that I was now a married woman and no longer daddy's little girl didn't hit me until the father-daughter dance at my reception. Tears ran down my face as we danced. Without my having to explain the tears, dad held me tight and whispered in my ear. "You'll always be my little girl."

I've been blessed that my parents live downstairs from me. They have had the opportunity to be a daily part of my now-adult children's lives. My dad never had a little boy, but I've given him two grandsons to pass his knowledge to. I've also given him two granddaughters he has chosen to spoil just like he did me. It's been an honor and privilege to watch my daddy be a wonderful Poppi to my children.

As my father has aged, health problems have stolen so much of his strength. I sat by his hospital bed as he fought for his every breath. My husband has held me in his arms while I've cried, praying dad would pull through, knowing I'm not ready to say goodbye. Thankfully, he's fought his way back and although most days are a struggle for him, battling pain and breathing issues, my hero is still alive and fighting.

The woman I am today is in great part due to the man who is my father. An example of bravery in the face of fear, willingness to help during times of trouble, and unconditional love no matter what the circumstance. I only hope that in my life I've made my daddy proud of the little girl he raised.

With much love ~Gumpie

IN BREVITY IS LOVE

Sewit Mesfen
Las Vegas, Nevada

"Santa Claus is not real." My father spoke firmly and without patience.

He looked at me through the thick lenses of aviator eyeglasses. I'd become enamored with a seeming religious icon. Santa Claus had been introduced to me in school earlier in the day. The other children seemed to revere him like a part of the Holy Trinity. An omniscient man with a *very* specific appearance who gifted children their heart's desire every year. How could my parents, who took me to church every Sunday and hung across not only on the inside but on the balcony of our Sunnyvale apartment, not inform me of his existence?

"Papa, but Jenny told me he brings her gifts every year."

My father raised his hand to his brow with exasperation. "Do not question." Taking a bite of his himbasha he continued, "Your American classmates need to believe he exists, but he is a tale. Their parents bring them gifts just as your mother and I do for you."

Having overheard my question, my mother finished bringing the afternoon tea to the table. "Why guale!" She laughed at my confusion, "Don't tell your classmates that Claus is not real."

My father sipped his steaming red tea, "Drink your sha'hee and complete some maths."
Most days off from school meant that I spent my days with my Mormon babysitter and her four children, learning to stay out of the way of the constant movement of a homemaker with a full house. But on a few lucky days, I accompanied my father to his office. I listened intently from my corner as he gave the newly emigrated advice on fitting in and succeeding in their new country.

"So, you are a German engineer, Mr. Herrmann. Why come here?"

I watched Mr. Herrmann struggle with the proper English words, "I wanted to get far away from home."

If my father wanted to be welcoming, he didn't show it. He flipped through the pages of his client's file, already memorized. The silence felt heavy as he sat, legs crossed, behind a wooden desk. He tapped on his thick mustache and looked up at Mr. Herrmann, who began to fidget nervously under the watchful gaze of his interrogator. Questions had ceased but it was clear that Mr. Herrmann was still being evaluated. Plenty of questions were being answered under a perceptive gaze.
Unable to withstand the tension further, "Mr. Mesfen, I am not a criminal. I simply need a new life."

A glass of water appeared to almost evaporate onto the desk. "Mr. Herrmann, I attended private schooling in Austria maybe 20 years after the war. I understand the area. But Germany can only flourish now." Without looking away, "Sewit, what was the date of Unification?"

I searched my mental history book, "October 3, 1990."
Mr. Herrmann nodded. "I will help you but perfekt Ihr Englisch oder Amerikaner werden Sie nicht ernst nehmen."

"Mr. Mesfen, your German is perfect!"

Though he dismissively raised his hand, it's just okay. I knew better. He spoke multiple languages flawlessly, struggling only with Mandarin for lack of practical use. While I loved my mom dearly, it was my father that I most related to. I didn't understand my mom's whimsy for fashion or makeup. A need for knowledge was alive in my father. Not in his heart — he would despise anyone using such a floral analogy — but in the cerebrum. Books were just as addictive to him as his Marlboro Reds. Though he judged fiction to be frivolous, non-fiction literature, especially those of the sciences, lined our home and his office.

Mr. Herrmann looked pointedly at the book in my own hands. It was the <u>Guide to Learning Tigrinya</u>.
Without the question, "I need my daughter to revise our language. Lest she forgets it around her classmates."
Mr. Herrmann nodded, "Do you teach her all of your culture?"

I nodded while my father flipped from page to page in the file, jotting down notes and circling information.

"Do you teach her futbol?" his client pressed.

"She plays with the girls and boys in her grade. She is no good," my father said plainly.

"What do you mean? Why do you not teach her? Maybe she struggles because she plays with boys."

"A girl can do anything as well as a boy. If she cannot figure out what she's doing wrong, then she should not play the sport."

This was a matter of fact. On game days he would stand disapprovingly on the sidelines as I fumbled a goal or failed to guard. My coach would take me aside and try to give me encouraging words, "It's okay, you're a fast runner but you need to work on aim." Or in the case of a defensive failure, "he simply out dribbled you, that's all." But it didn't matter. I could feel the eyes of a disapproving father expecting me to self-correct.

When giving him my report card, I would wait in agony as his eyes would skim the line of tent-shaped letters knowing he would arrive at the unsatisfactory "A-" and scold me for failing myself. Unsure of where to begin in that glaringly weak subject I would simply begin again, re-reading and re-memorizing until I was sure there would be nothing to chastise on the next round of report cards.

"Mr. Herrmann, this is your file. Revise it, complete it *accurately* and bring it back to me at your next appointment. Remember what I said, perfect your English."

It became clear to me over time that neither of my parents earned much money in their respective careers, or at least not enough to justify living in now-gentrified Sunnyvale. When I began having growth spurts my father would sigh relegating some money to "just a few" new clothes. When we suffered infestations, my mother would calm my father's nerves by coating our floorboards with vinegar. When the late summer season cast waves of heat over Silicon Valley my parents would opt to turn on all the fans and open the windows and doors. A far cry from my friends' lavishly air-conditioned homes.

I'm not sure, then, why it came as a surprise when my parents announced they had purchased a house in Las Vegas and that we would move in less than two weeks.
A bit of social isolation and a lack of family adventuring plagued us after our relocation. Weekends that had once been filled with trips into the city with cousins, or get-togethers with fellow Eritreans, were replaced with work. In a 24/7 city, my parents found themselves buckled down to work weekends to accommodate our new lives. I was just thrilled to finally live in a house and attend a high school in which I could reinvent myself. My six-year-old brother was ecstatic to have a yard and spoke nonstop about the possibilities of a dog. My mother settled into work graveyard and my father began an unfulfilling career as a cab driver.

My father and I didn't speak for a few years following my parents' divorce. Not because I was angered by their separation but rather because I had supported my mother's emancipation from a man who drank heavily enough to bury his own life's disappointments. A man for whom I'd called an ambulance when a night of heavy drinking resulted in a fall and head injury. A man who slurred hateful things towards me in a thinly veiled resentment that I was not and, probably, would not become the daughter he had hoped for.

My father had taken it as an affront to his very being when I told him it would be best that my brother did not grow up in a turbulent home. Or that I pointed out that neither he nor my mother had appeared happy in some years predating the relocation to Las Vegas.

In a stubborn refusal of admission, he simply ceased communication. At first, I didn't understand what was happening. When my calls would lead to voicemail, I reasoned he was busy at work, unable to answer with passengers in his cab. After all, how unprofessional would it look to tourists if their cab driver wasn't paying attention to the road? Or maybe, I would convince myself, he's just at home sleeping or away from his cell phone. After all, how many times had I seen him put his cell phone down and walk away? He was never fond of technology.

When the wave of parental rejection rose overhead and came crashing upon me in an incessant force of grief, I denied it. I was sad because my university course load was exhausting. I was just a bit down because my unfulfilling warehouse job was never-ending.

Then came the anger.

"How could he be so selfish!" I yelled in my mother's home. "Why can't he think of anyone but himself? I hate him!"

My mother placed her hands flat on the dining room table. As though pressing her palms would reveal the secret to calming her eldest from a fit of rage.

"Your father loves you, he just…" her voice trailed as her eyes shifted to the corner of the room resting on a patterned, hand-woven mesob. Almost addressing the mesob she continued, "He has some problems but there is nothing he loves more than his children. Just because he can't express it, doesn't mean it's not there. Don't hate him."

A few years later, on a peculiarly cold Vegas day, I received a text message. It read simply: Call me, Dad. In the true reflection of my father, I wanted to leave the message unanswered. I held all his best qualities. Why shouldn't I also embrace the flaws genetically ingrained in half of my DNA? Could I not deny the accidental feminist who raised me with the knowledge that I could forever better myself? He'd been my driving force and the very educator who helped poise me to sit on the precipice of adulthood victory, a pending home purchase. Was it unfair to say that I would find more success removing him from my life?

I attempted to get to know him. The real him, in a way that had been promised to me by my peers or therapists, "Oh parents start to open up as they age." He would only ever budge in centimeters. Instead, dropping small crumbs of what comprised his full recipe. "In the war, I dumped sugar in my gas tank so my enemies couldn't use it as I escaped," he would say without prompting. Or once, "I've never used a gun, but I have used many knives." But his response to further questions was oftentimes a hand, palm facing me.

Sometimes I would receive snippets of his childhood, "When your grandfather sent me to school in Europe, he did not expect me to return to join the war efforts."

"So why did you return?"

"Sometimes you don't need questions."

"How did you and Mom meet?" A story that, to this day, neither has been told.

This was always where he shut down. "She no longer exists."

And the questions that I could never ask; Why did you ever have kids? Do you have kids that I don't know about? Could you ever tell me you're proud of me? They die on my lips without the courage to ask them and I convince myself I don't need to know. Sometimes you don't need questions.

These days I pick up the phone when he calls. A static-filled call from Eritrea, "Sewit how are you."

"I'm good Dad, how are you?"

"Great, how is your brother, work, health?"

"All of it is excellent. How is retirement and home"

"Fine."

"That's good."

"I miss you; I'll call you again soon."

"I miss you too, I love you."

"I love you too."

Our routine. Brief, but I know he's all right and it gives me peace.

HERO, UNDEFINED

Julie Isaacson
Highland Park, Illinois

"We were happy because we knew who we were."
--Paul Halpern

Not a day or night passes without acknowledging my good fortune in having won the dad lottery. I'm the only person who has the distinction of calling this exemplary man my father. I feel a bit selfish about that, as I wish every person could have had the benefit of this father, mentor, advisor, coach, partner, role model, and overall friend.

In the past 25 years since he suddenly passed away, I've spent countless hours analyzing what combination of qualities made him so special. He was unique to many people, not just me, and I continue to hear fresh and heartening stories about him and the impact he had on innumerable lives. What characteristics melded in this man to have created such a legacy?

I've concluded that like so much of life, striking the right balance is key to every endeavor, and maximizing a healthy heart, soul, and body. Dad's outlook and perspective provided him an unparalleled sense of humor, with wisdom to know when the occasion indicated serious attention. He was able to see both the forest and the trees. He was a shrewd businessman, and his sense of timing could determine when a person might need advice, or when he needed to gently guide with a few well-placed questions, which could lead to one's own smart conclusions. Dad was a savvy man who could sense what a person needed before they even knew it, or could express it, for themselves.

Having the privilege of being his daughter allowed me to interact with him every day, as well as observe him as he made it his life's passion to help take on a load of another person. He wore his patience as easily as he fit customers with perfect shoes for their foot. He engaged people from all walks of life, all ages, all races, with universal respect, admiration, and interest.

As a storyteller, I recently shared a loving memory about my dad that illustrates his whimsy and caring. When purging my parents' home a few years ago, I came across my 4th-grade project requiring the collection of different species of LEAVES. Fifty years after the fact, I could close my eyes and distinctly recall the day my parents and I had undertaken this event. A typical week for my father was working in his store ten hours a day, Monday through Saturday. On Sunday, the hours were reduced to four. I had Sunday School, and while Mom was making salmon patties for lunch, he rested for a half-hour, and I gathered my bags, tape, and scissors. After lunch, we ventured across the Mississippi River from my town to Davenport, Iowa, where a park offered up a hundred species of trees. I snipped and labeled it neatly. Then, I spotted the gorgeous ginkgo tree and coveted leaves beyond my reach from my little stool. Dad tried and couldn't quite reach them, either. Mom was ready to give up and find another tree, but Dad regarded my face. He steadily hoisted me up into the tree, balancing me with confidence and strength, holding only my feet, while my lanky ten-year-old legs allowed me to reach overhead for the delicate, green trophy. The look on his face showed such love and a feeling of accomplishment. That was his customary look—purpose, light-hearted pride, and achievement-- which I now recalled as I held these dehydrated brittle leaves, with brown tape to match. I closely held special memories of who and what once lived.

The year following the leaves project brought terrible flooding of the Mississippi River, one of the worst in the history of the Quad Cities of Illinois and Iowa. The basement of Dad's store was at risk of flooding, as were the homes of the clerks who worked for him. He insisted they all go home to attend to their own lives. Single-handedly, he scaled the store's cellar steps dozens of times, to salvage whatever merchandise he could. He stacked some sandbags, to help in whatever fractional way they could. That night, exhausted, he listened to the news, learning that the high schools had canceled classes the next day, as teenagers were at the riverfront sandbagging at a furious pace. Dad suddenly gained a second wind. With my mom, they went to the supermarket and came home with enough ingredients to make hundreds of sandwiches to take to the river to fuel the kids. It was late, and they wouldn't let me make the delivery with them as I still had school the next day—but I could read the sense of satisfaction my dad wore, knowing our family had put forth an extra effort to help others. I was happy to hear they'd been met with cheers from the starving teens.

My dad was the shoulder and ear I turned to first throughout my life. He always knew the right thing to say or to NOT say, during challenging times. He had the vision to muster guidance that allowed me to make clear and purposeful decisions. One example was when I was trying to weigh whether to attend graduate school as planned or take a teaching job that had suddenly become available. I still recall the series of questions he asked me that helped me clarify that the job was the better choice, and that decision launched a career I've enjoyed for 40 years. As he'd predicted, graduate school came later, at a time when I had some real-life experience under my belt.

It was my dad who was the first to help me maneuver through the fault lines in my starter marriage and offer support in any way he could. He helped me accept my decisions and taught me to not second-guess. He exhibited unwavering strength and knew exactly how to transfer it. While he was no longer living at the time of the collapse of my long-time marriage, I continued to feel his wisdom guiding me through the choppy waters.

Within the last couple of years, a long-time colleague of my dad's called me just to chat and shared with me that he got his start in business due to my dad's encouragement. The man said, "sometimes I'd get so frustrated about decisions I had to make, I'd call your father and say, 'Just tell me what to do and I'll do it. I just can't decide.' Your Dad would listen to me, and then say, 'I'm happy to discuss the options with you, but I can't tell you what to do because what's right for me might not be right for you.' I always came to a clear path after talking to him."

I've learned more insights about my father over the past couple of years, having discovered hundreds of letters written during WW2 between him and his parents and four siblings in Illinois. He didn't complain or dwell on hardships in training, or in Germany, where he served as a sergeant in the Timberwolves division. He asked questions about what was going on in their lives. He shared anecdotes peppered with his humor that were surely a nice distraction stateside to counteract their worry. The message in the letters is loud and clear. Family first. Love first. Acting on what was right according to a high moral code made nothing else matter. Choices and decision-making were clear when not clouded by flimsy factors that weren't part of his manifesto.

When I was a young child, I remember reading a book at the table, where my dad was writing out some checks. I'd noticed his signature. Paul H. Halpern. "Daddy, I didn't know you had a middle name. What is it?" He smiled at me a little sheepishly, "Honey, I don't have a middle name. When I was young, my friends all had middle names, which they signed with an initial. I thought it looked official, and I decided to use a middle initial, too. I picked an H."

At his 80th birthday party, just two months before he unexpectedly passed away, I told the story and described what I felt the H stood for. Of course, top of the list was his Humor, to which everyone who knew him could attest. I feel blessed that he passed that on to me, and people appreciate it the same way his audience of one or more benefited from his. His H stood for Honesty. I knew if I talked to him about any topic, big or small, that his response would be steeped in his sincere, genuine, open perspective. I observed him in thousands of interactions in his store, giving true opinions, not just to make a sale, but to support people in being their best. His honesty led to the formation of trusting relationships. Another H for my dad's initials is that of Hero--to me, to my children, who were very young when he died, and to all who knew him. He had the qualities that people yearn for in heroes. Men of his caliber are few and far between.

Humility was another of my father's hallmarks. He never took anything or anyone for granted. He honored his roots, and even in building a successful life, never forgot them, or minimized them. At my father's funeral, my mother and I were in a state of shock, and I still recall looking out over the hundreds of people who attended. I remember saying to my mother, "The words we hear today aren't going to matter as much as what you are looking at. Look at his legacy." There were the faces of old and young, every shade of black, brown, yellow, and white, every religion, Catholic, Jewish, Christian, Jehovah's Witness, every economic class from poor to wealthy. All to pay their respects to a man who showed every one of them equal respect. Standing in front of them made me feel prouder than I had ever felt. All through my life, he had made me feel adored and lucky to be his daughter. And now at the end of his life, that pride emanated over the entire group of family, friends, and acquaintances who had been befriended, assisted, honored, and acknowledged by Paul.

I'm grateful to have had the foresight 30 years ago to do an oral autobiography interview with my dad, about his life. While he didn't care for the spotlight, he agreed to do it, and the recording is my most prized possession. During the interview, I asked him about the impact of certain life events in their family and being in a religious minority in a small town. His response describes exactly how he viewed his life, his simple code of moral ethics, and his ability to live a life of impeccable standards. His response: "We were happy because we knew who we were." This is wisdom to live by from the wisest of men. When people comment to me that "I'm my father's daughter," I could not possibly feel more honored, more touched, or more humbled. His are hard shoes to fill. And I'll spend all my life trying to keep them fitting as snugly as his memorable hugs.

A GIFT FOR DAD

Michelle Spencer
Pompton Lakes, New Jersey

I can see another bus pulling into the stop. My eyes open wider, and I scan each passenger as they step onto the platform; no, he isn't on that one. I was about seven years old, standing on the baseboard looking out of the window waiting for my father to get off the bus to come to visit me.

My parents had been divorced for as long as I can remember and for him to come to visit me, he had to take a bus to New York Port of Authority, then a connecting bus to my house. He has good intentions, however many times he never makes it out of the pub from New York to my bus.

Hours would go by, and I wouldn't leave my post, knowing with conviction he would be on the next bus. My mother checked in at random times, trying her best to coax me from the window, but to no avail. Eventually, a quietness shrouds the bus stop, there are no more people waiting, and no more busses pulling in, the night was over.

My mother worked as a secretary for Burt Bacharach in Midtown; the theatre was always in her blood, and my father was in construction working on Manhattan's skyscrapers. They met, fell in love, got married at City Hall, then the stork delivered me into their world. Mom was thrilled, dad was also thrilled but not mature enough to be a father. By my second birthday, she had kicked him out and decided to raise me on her own.

School breaks were spent with my father, where he would take me to all the museums in New York, the Planetarium to see the Rockettes and my favorite Ringling Bros Circus. I always knew my father loved me, he simply wasn't present in my life growing up, except to whirl in and out when he managed to catch graduation or birthday.

Dad remarried six years later and gave me the gift of four sisters. From the very beginning, the word stepsister or half-sister was never part of our vocabulary. Dad was more present with my sisters, at the tender age of forty he was finally ready to grow up.

Our relationship stayed the same, we saw each other on holidays and special occasions where we engaged in superficial conversation and an obligatory kiss on the forehead.

I had harbored much anger and resentment for my father for many years for not being there for me growing up, and for my mother having to raise and support me on her own. My mother passed away a week after my eighteenth birthday. She had gotten the news she had cancer with six months to live which turned into three weeks. I was young, and confused, sitting in an ICU room and my aunt and dad came right to the hospital. My dad was there when she passed, he went home with me and helped me with the funeral arrangements. I was still so angry deep inside, I refused to allow him to be a pallbearer at her funeral.

Life took a turn like a kite caught in a wind gust after I married and had children, suddenly he was involved and excited. Dad would ask me to bring them down for the weekend and he had treats, took them to the boardwalk and even the beach! The beautiful thing was it was natural; I didn't know what came over him and he didn't realize it either until one day it hit him. My oldest was about three and my younger gal was about one and I was picking them up from a weekend with him.

My youngest, who was not mobile when I dropped her off, suddenly let go of the chair and took about five steps right into grandpa's arms! I gasped in delight and just screamed "she took her first steps!" Dad sat back and he gazed off and I could see his eyes begin to water with sadness. Still off in a gaze, he said, "You know, I was never there for any of your "firsts," I missed them all."

Suddenly all the anger and resentment and punishing feelings I had melted away. The look of sadness on his face was more painful than anything I had ever seen; he was truly remorseful and hurt by his actions.

Two years later he thought he pulled a muscle in his chest, He called me, and I met him at the hospital. No pulled muscle, but they found a mass that looked "questionable," which turned out to be cancer.

Luckily, they were able to cut it out without any chemo or radiation, it was a long and brutal six months.

He was frightened and I seemed to be the only one that could calm him. I began to manage his healthcare and every night after my husband at the time would come home from work, I would pick him up a coffee and jelly ring and drive the sixty miles to the hospital and we would watch Jeopardy and Wheel of Fortune, then he would go to bed, and I would go home.

I realized I could not sustain his outpatient follow-ups being so far away, so I convinced him to move in with me until an opening in the Senior Housing became available.

It was then that we became inseparable; he went everywhere with me. Dad went with me food shopping, to pick the children up at school, he even finagled his way to accompany me to a job interview! I would come home from work, and he would have my pajamas laid out and a cup of hot tea waiting for me and then together we would watch our two favorite game shows and call it a night.

Fast forward twenty years. Dad was now living in the Senior Housing, my marriage had failed, and we divorced, and even though dad didn't follow me around anymore, we still faithfully had Sunday dinners at my house and tea during the week at his.

Healthwise his cancer came back two more times, the second one was treated with radiation which burned him, and the doctors sat us down and told us blatantly, "it's not a matter of *if* the cancer comes back, it is when it does. You are not a candidate for chemotherapy or radiation, so unless it is a mass and we can successfully cut it out, we are out of options. We strongly suggest you enjoy every day as if it is a gift."

And that he did. He was the life of the party, a handful, politically incorrect, blunt without a filter, and unapologetic for anything he said or did, and he did it with conviction. At 6-foot two, baby blue eyes, charismatic charm, and an incredulous wit. He could make you laugh and shake your head at the same time.

His escapades have gotten us thrown out of shopping stores and convenience stores and there was the third grade bring your grandfather school day that didn't turn out so well when he dropped the *F-bomb* a few times because Johnny wasn't reading fast enough and told the teacher she had nice boobs.

He appreciated the time he had left and made the most out of it every second he could with each of us. Every month the entire family got together and celebrated birthdays and special occasions. This man would pull holidays out of a hat for an excuse so that we all could be together and enjoy each other's company.

I began to write a column about him to share the adventures in our world titled "Out of the mouth of Bob." Dad became a popular character on an online website and was loved by a lot of people. Writing is cathartic for me and sharing stories about him to the world made me happy, I relived each escapade through every word. It fueled my passion to write.

I told him about it about six months into the column, and being the ham that he is, he simply laughed and couldn't believe that I was writing about him. Sadly, dad never got to read any of the columns, he didn't have the Internet and I never printed out any of the columns because I was busy, and I thought we'd catch up later.

I took him for his regular checkups, made sure his pacemaker was up to date, his ultrasounds and scans were done on time. Dad didn't understand the medical world, nor did he have any desire to learn it, he just pointed to me and said she'll handle it, tell me what to do and I'll do it.

I started dating a man, Mark, and almost instantly there was a connection between the two. The first Sunday dinner question shifted from "what are you making?" to "is my man coming?" That was the nickname he gave Mark and he beamed if he knew Mark would be at dinner or anywhere, we were.

It was during one of dad's emergency room visits, the nurse was fiddling with the monitors and Mark walked in to see him. Dad looked up at the nurse and said, "this is my son, Mark." Little did we know that we would receive the news that the hospital stays that cancer had returned and dad had about six months to live.

Dad's 75th birthday was a week away and we had planned a big party for him with the entire family, partly because it was a milestone and because we all knew it would be the last birthday he would celebrate.

On the eve of his birthday, Mark asked my father for my hand in marriage. Dad told him he was crazy and ran for the hills as fast as he could. That was dad code for congratulations, welcome to the family. It wasn't just a proposal; Mark had spent the past weeks planning a wedding. He had the date, venue and guest list all planned out and told me all I had to do was take care of dad and show up.

Mark wanted my father to not only know that his daughter would be taken care of, but he wanted him to be there and part of it. Dad was overjoyed and grateful for a gift that Mark never knew he gave dad…a second chance. An opportunity to be present for his daughter's wedding, unlike the first time where he was not.

Never underestimate the power of a chance to make things right before you take your last breath. We married in the hospital chapel and my father's eyes were filled with joy and peace. He could move on with complete resolve and without any regrets. In the middle of the ceremony, Mark had placed his communion cross ring on dad's finger and told him that the ring would stay with him on the other side. My father, who is rarely moved, for the first time, began to cry, tears of joy and grace.

I am an emotional blocker. When sad or bad things happen, I block them out so that I can continue to function as a wife, mother, and employee. The day he passed was the last day I wrote. My subject was gone and as much as I tried to write about other times we had, I simply had no words, I felt dead inside; the fire that once burned bright with creativity now lay somewhere buried in the thick smoldering smoke.

These are the first words I have put to paper in nine months. It had me dig deep inside and unblock memories. Some sentences were met with tears, others a smile, some erased altogether, but all helped rip down a piece of the emotional blockade and I feel lighter. Dad, this one's for you.

LOST TIME

Wendy Toth Notarnicola
Long Valley, New Jersey

When I was very little, my dad was my protector. He was the one I'd run to when I was afraid, had a nightmare, or got hurt. I felt safe and protected in his arms, but somewhere along the way, that changed, and my mother was the cause.

My dad was a good father. He worked hard–sometimes working late hours, but he would always come into our room when he got home, kiss us, and make sure we were tucked in. He never missed a day of work, never missed a mortgage payment or bill, and he always put food on the table and clothing on our backs. Above all, he was never abusive in any way to any of us, including my mother. Despite this, my mother, who would later be diagnosed with a narcissistic personality disorder, would constantly find reasons to pick a fight with him. It was so common that I could tell it was going to be a "fight night" by the way her back would stiffen when she heard his car coming up the driveway. I used to feel so sad for my father when coming home after a hard day's work, and she'd start screaming at him out of nowhere. In contrast to her stiffened back, his shoulders would noticeably droop.

Soon, my mother started brainwashing us. We didn't recognize it as brainwashing at the time, but it was.

She used to tell us that he acted sweet and loving to us, but he was violent, and he was going to kill us all one day. I was so confused, why would our father want to kill us? We'd never experienced anything but love from him.

One day, before Dad came home, Mom made us barricade our bedroom door by pushing our bunk beds against it. She said we had to do that to protect ourselves because he was going to hurt us that night. We protested, but my mother insisted, so we would comply and help her push the bunk beds across the door. When he got home, he tried to get in for goodnight kisses but found himself blocked. He asked what was wrong, but we didn't answer, so he pushed so hard he managed to open the door. Bizarrely, my mother played innocent and said, "Oh, I thought you were a burglar breaking in," and quietly left the room with Dad.

This same scene was repeated for several more weeks, and my father started to grow suspicious when she'd act innocent and come up with some excuse about hearing a noise earlier or getting a prank phone call that scared her. If he pushed too hard, though, she'd start a fight, so he just clammed up.

About that time, I started having nightmares and biting my nails–a habit I carry with me to this day. One day, as he was trying to push through the barricade, she threw open the window and whispered to us to jump, because she was sure he had a knife.

It was a cold winter night, and we were in pajamas with bare feet. We jumped out of our first-floor window onto the frozen pavement, and she joined us and told us to start running until we were out of view of our house. We walked around for what felt like hours, shivering, and crying, begging to go back, barely able to feel our feet, but she said no, that we couldn't go back until he left for church in the morning. For at least an hour, we dodged my father's car–he'd been searching the neighborhood for us, but we kept to the backyards, where he couldn't see us. We wound up circling back and sleeping in the vestibule of the neighboring house, praying that the neighbors wouldn't wake up and find us there.

Finally, about seven in the morning, we heard my father's car start up and saw it drive down the block and out of sight. We collapsed, exhausted, onto our beds, and slept for hours.

After she grew bored with the barricade game, she started leaving knives in our room with pictures of us with our heads cut off. She told us Dad had done that as a warning–he was getting closer to killing us. I could hardly sleep at all during this period. The brainwashing had begun to work on us. She no longer had to make us barricade our bedroom door; we had started to believe he would kill us one day. We'd answer in one or two-word sentences when he'd ask about our day, about school and homework, etc. After a while, he gave up, and dinner time was generally silent. I can't imagine how hurt he must have felt during that time, and I feel nothing but shame when I think about how I allowed myself to be brainwashed.

Somewhere between our preteen and teen years, the brainwashing wore off and we began talking to Dad again, dealing with Mom's hateful punishments as best as we could. I escaped the madness when I went off to college, and Dad would come to visit me and we'd talk, have lunch, and try to make up for the lost time. On weekends and holidays, I'd stay at my boyfriend's parents' house and Dad would sneak off to see me.

When I started having children, I would invite Dad over every weekend so he could spend time with the kids. Watching him with the babies was amazing–he was such a natural. He loved holding them in his arms, rocking them, and feeding them. Distant memories flooded back of how he'd cuddle with me and my sisters, read to us, comb our hair, and make us breakfast. Dad even came to my community orchestra concerts. When I was a child, his job didn't allow him to take off and come to school plays and concerts; seeing him in the audience beaming at me proudly made me feel like a little girl again.

When I'd ask my dad why he never left my mother, he'd say, "I was basically blackmailed. She told me she'd take you, girls, away and I'd never see you again. I was too afraid to take that chance."

My father passed away three years ago and I'm so happy that we were able to make up for the lost time and that my children got to know him, play with him at the park, and go for ice cream with him on weekends. I am glad that when he was in hospice care I got to feed him, brush his teeth, comb his hair, and be there for him like he'd been there for me and my sisters. On his last day, he couldn't speak anymore, but he reached for my hand, held it tightly, and wouldn't let go. We may have been cheated out of a lot of time together, but I am so grateful that I got to hold his hand and gaze into his eyes until he closed them for the last time.

PIECES OF MY FATHER

Ya'el Chaikind
Santa Fe, New Mexico

My father's imprint branded my spirit when I was six years old, the day he left without saying goodbye. It was a classic abandonment story embedded in the deep recesses of my lizard brain, and despite 40 years dedicated to rewriting the tale, today, ripe with 56 years of experience, I cede defeat. These tidal forces dragged me along the currents of my life, ebbing and flowing, but never really moving from the same few feet of sand, rubbed raw over time.

The aging film of this first six years clatters in black and white, a tattered glimpse into those early days. Excitedly hiding from him in the oversized chair as he trudged up the stairs with the morning light, home after his night shift, I would yell "Boo!" Sharing a whole watermelon, just the two of us with messy, juicy smiles. Kicking me under the table during dinner for no reason, beginning a lifelong nervous tic in my eye. Squeezing my hand so hard I crumbled to my little girl knees while he smiled and said, "What?"

Most nights I crouched in the corner of my room, rocking while plugging my ears. I hummed to drown out the apocalyptic yelling as my father's deep voice shouted epithets at my mother. My mother also played this game that no one won. They volleyed violent screams and threats through the thin apartment walls. Frequently dishes crashed against the living room wall shared by my bedroom. The sounds tore apart my chest. Occasionally neighbors called the police.

"It's all my fault, it's all my fault!" shrieked the stories in my head. Cliché noted, yet my formidable thinking brain was no match for the ancient mandate to survive at all costs. Hypervigilant, I was ready to seek out and protect myself from danger real or imagined. Fight. Men's voices and loud noises scared me. Fright.

In romantic relationships I offered and then walled off trust and love in preparation for sudden abandonment. These relationships became a slow death, bleeding by a thousand tiny pinpricks until I could not stand the ambivalent dissonance and left. Flight.

My wound was so well notated it had footnotes, references, and a detailed table of contents. Regardless of this vast clarity, a huge sense of self-responsibility for my choices, and promises to myself to do it differently, I managed to keep choosing men like my father. Stuck on a gerbil wheel, I choked on the karmic seed in my throat by recreating this abandonment story over and over. Freeze.

Birthday cards and Sunday forays with my father ended when I was about 12. When I was 16, I spent a year trying to find the light in my father's darkness after he ripped his shirt, Jewishly declaring my older sister dead after an argument over her wedding, to which he was not invited. I yearned to understand how I was my father's daughter and searched for any guideposts and benefits of the doubt to overcome his years of emotional and physical absence. With innocent hope, I asked my father to spend time with me, transparently telling him that I wished to get to know him.

We went for walks in nature with his camera. Fed Wasa crackers to giraffes at the zoo because who else would eat them? Shared many Chinese dinners after a movie, shadows of the few years post-divorce. When someone took our parking space, my father jumped out of the car swearing and banged on the other guy's windshield while I sank low in my seat so no one could tell I was with him.

He sent me a subscription to Reader's Digest, to him a quality journalism outlet, and told me stupid puns while we ate cake in Jersey diners where he knew all the waitresses because he had no other place to go. There were some diners where my father was no longer welcome, based on boorish arguments with customers or staff. Because of his union contract, instead of being fired he was transferred to many different grocery stores over his 20-plus year career, due to insubordination and fights. To my surprise, he wondered aloud what would have happened if he and my mother had gone to a counselor.

My father spied a building that had recently caught fire and we went searching through the smoking remains for treasures. He jangled his many coins and keys in his pocket as he walked. In his wallet was a paper with the grave markers for the Jewish cemetery where his parents were buried. His anger singed his words and spittle flew when he spoke about my mother and most other people in his life, all of whom had taken advantage of him in various ways. Racial slurs vented through him unapologetically.

After a year I decided that whatever light might have resided in his cigarette-tinged coffee breath was no longer there. I retreated under my mother's roof, reluctantly acquiescing to her longstanding tirade against my father though hip to how her own rage co-created this story. Only much later would I appreciate the mixed bag of fear and love that comprises each of us and propels our stories forward, for better or worse.

At 26, a psychic took one look at me and said, "Your father has abandoned you in every lifetime." She did not know me, and my jaw dropped as she named this shameful secret I tried mightily to hide from the world. I stuck my fingernail in my thumb to avoid sobbing with this acknowledgement that opened a dark hidden cave inside of me. It was the first time my father's legacy contacted fresh air and I was not quite sure what to do as this raw, oozing feeling leaked out. Anxious, I tried to shove my unlovableness and unworthiness back into their hole but there was no going back. I imagined it all left a slimy trail behind me, for all to see. I wanted to disappear.

On the way home from the psychic, I stopped at the car inspection station, and as I left they slapped a big red "Rejection" sticker on my window for a burnt taillight. I drove away but soon needed to stop because I was laughing and crying at the same time. Was I really rejected because my car was rejected? Was I really rejected because my father left?

For a moment, this giddy revelation smoothed a few ragged edges, and over ensuing years I continued to achieve measures of insight and healing that truly seemed to add up. I developed mastery at finding the shards of light in other people's darkness and learned to love that light instead of focusing on their more difficult qualities. Yet I kept choosing relationships with people who had an abundance of darkness, with whom I had to search for their light constantly. I wondered if this quest had become a surrogate for love, a game of catch and release embedded in my abandoned heart as a remnant from my father. I wondered if it would be better to choose someone with lighter and learn to love their slivers of darkness instead.

"The gift lies next to the wound," chant sages, gurus, and modern mystics, and I began to shine a light into the corners of my own darkness, ready for a heroine's journey in my 40s. I fasted on a vision quest, confronted a waking vision of my father, and watched his spirit fly like a hawk above the red desert rocks, free at last from his burdens. Over a decade of forgiveness rituals offered small steps towards my own freedom as the enigma of paternal lost love started to loosen its grip on me. The magical thinking of my childhood transformed into reality as I saw more clearly the mere human behind the man that was my father.

For years I did not hear from my father, nor even know where he was living, until a veteran's hospital in

North Carolina tracked me down to tell me he was dying, and did I want to come see him? When I got to the hospital, I noticed he still had a full head of thick hair, even in his 70s. Ammonia from his cancer gave him a type of dementia, and he talked to me as if I was my mother or my sister. His lips were chapped, and I put balm on them, one of the only times I physically touched my father since childhood. He died a week later, and I was sent his belongings: An ancient camera, a folded American flag, and his wallet. Pieces of a life that I never fathomed.

Sifting through the burnt remains of my own life, I realized I had been searching for fragments of my father my entire life. I never gave up the dream that I would find him, like buried treasure. Even if covered in soot, I would polish his scratches into a jewel, watching him transform into my hero. I searched for pieces of my father to retrieve pieces of myself, to create a collage that told a new story where I felt whole at last. Perhaps a dose of magical thinking was requisite to transform the past into a present worth living.

About ten years after my father's death, I stepped onto the path of my Jewish ancestors. I read that a soul could not rest unless the *Kaddish*, the Mourner's Prayer, was said for them. Much time had passed, and I realized no one had ever said this prayer for my father. Many said kind words about their loved ones after reciting *Kaddish*, yet I did not want to be inauthentic. Suddenly, I knew what to say: "Thank you for my life today. May your memory be a blessing."

The truth was right in front of me the entire time. No longer blinded by pain, I understood. I *was* my father's daughter. I love giraffes, because they have the biggest hearts of all land mammals and are the symbol of nonviolent communication. I once was hired as the only white girl in a Chinese restaurant because I could name every ingredient in every dish on the menu. Movies and photos are my main art forms, and I love to hike in nature. Diner food is a main attraction, stupid jokes are my specialty, and whenever I eat watermelon, I think of him.

The dark echoes of my father often translate to feeling broken, discarded, and left behind, and sometimes I still struggle to live more in my light than in my darkness. Yet I am adept at finding these pockets of light everywhere because they are illuminated against the black backdrop of my life story. As a result of this journey, I have a gift for helping others find ways out of their darkness. I use my father's legacy to help people shine light into murky corners to retrieve their hidden treasures so that they can learn to be the heroes and heroines of their own lives.

PARTED VANISHED

Jenny Nash
London, England

My primary caregiver when growing up was my father. As a painter/schizophrenic, he was the best of playmates. His vivid imagination and heightened good moods made him the most exciting and fun person to play with. It was on his downward spirals, however, when his paranoia got the best of him. At these times things weren't quite as fun. He was never violent or aggressive, he never raised his voice. He was always gentle, always the most loving of my parents; he was never late to pick me up from school, no matter his headspace, which made me luckier than many. Then one day he wasn't there to pick me up.

My father passed away when I was nine, and the impact of this sudden parting of my playmate and the protector affected me into my teenage and adult life. A common thread that ties me to my father is that I was diagnosed with bipolar disorder (a branch off from schizophrenia). This may have been passed down to me from him. I self-medicated my mental health issues, blocking out the voices and the following trauma from my teenage years, with alcohol and other things. It was during that time that I made a pact with myself; to end my life and join the 27 club. I ran away to London in 2014 to pass the time until this fateful day, faking interest in BA Photography for the student finance money.

Photography had always been a part of my life: I had forever taken photographs and my journey of healing began with my introduction to Sigmund Freud's theory of "Pathography" by a photographer I once thought that I knew, Dr. Spencer Rowell. The word pathography was used by the psychoanalyst Sigmund Freud on the last page of his psychobiography of Leonardo da Vinci. Freud theorized that an analyst might examine the work of an artist and in doing so reveal something of their unconscious, internal world. After reading his book, I realized that he had broken many of his own rules for his psychobiography to be valid. A psychoanalyst, by profession, is objective, which requires emotional distance when they are with patients, so I am now strongly of the opinion that to put an artwork into that dyadic situation is to remove the potential for personal resonance and projection. In the last five years I have developed my methodology of "Auto-pathography," in which I leave a finished artwork for a time and then come back to it, audio recording a "session" with it, verbalizing what it speaks back to me of myself, though the artwork is the analyst and the self the analysand. A chemical imbalance in one's brain makes this an interesting process, and I'm not always sure that the voice I hear is my own.

After extensive research, I immersed myself in re-enactment phototherapy, which was originally developed by Rosy Martin and the late Jo Spence in the 1980s. It's important to say that Rosy, always kind and tolerant, has been very generous in giving her time and knowledge to me, advising me in the development of my work. She explained how Spence and she worked together, one taking the role of sitter/director, the other photographer/therapist to work on and through past traumas in their lives by re-enacting these in performative actions, and transforming them, whilst held and contained by the therapeutic gaze of the other. My sessions, however, are done solo, with a camera set to shoot continuously, all the while audio recording on my phone, capturing not only my image but the stream of unconscious narratives provoked by putting myself in these roles. This is not the true phototherapy developed by Martin and Spence, but a solo-phototherapy of sorts, which, coupled with Auto-Pathography, has become my tool for self-discovery, reflection, and healing. I recreated a school photograph of my father from when he was nine, trying to get back in touch with him, and, using these two images and a third of me when I was a child, I made a series of ten mixed-media Rorschach tests. These and other experiments can be viewed by searching #PartedVanishedSRP on Instagram.

In my deep depressive states, it is my practice (inspired by Rowell and Martin's work) that helps me move forward. I replace the dark voices in my head with the voices of the photographers I was taught by through my studies at London Met Arts. I am so lucky that they gave me the tools to fight, and a purpose to keep on living.

Mick Williamson, Susan Andrews, Zelda Cheatle, Heather McDonough, David George, Rod Morris, and others love, and care are the reason I am still here today. I bypassed the 27 club, turning 28 and graduating with a research MA, and it made me feel strong enough to challenge what I fear and help pass my experience on to others who are fighting with their heads daily. At this point, it is appropriate to acknowledge Dr. Rowell's influence on me also. After several years of projecting our unhealed trauma back and forth onto each other like fractious siblings, I parted ways with him under the most tragic reasons and under the most tragic circumstances.

In 2021, I was shortlisted for the New Emergence Art Prize for self-portraits recreating the rare visual hallucinations that come to me, to make them seem less real. The hallucinations, a common symptom of my father's paranoid schizophrenia, which is not always present in those with bipolar, are what I fear most.

My current auto-pathography project is an ongoing series which began in 2021, chronicling the recovery process from Narcissistic Victim Syndrome (a form of PTSD) which is a long process that I can only describe as an internal civil war. My greatest wish is to advance my work at Ph.D. level, to show the world we are not just our diagnosis. One day I will put my completed thesis on my bookshelf. This will be the acknowledgment to my father, that he was also more than his diagnosis. He was a son, a husband, and the greatest dad anyone could have been lucky enough to spend nine years with.

"The tragedy is you want your dad to see this but of course if he was here, he would never see this. That's the beautiful thing if it wasn't so tragic. The beautiful paradox of your life; you create this fantastic art because of what happened."
SPENCER ROWELL, 2017

MY FATHER'S DITTO

Gargi Mehra
India

One evening a company director, on the verge of retirement, stepped into the elevator in his office building. He found a group of his young colleagues engaged in noisy chatter. Upon questioning them, one lad said, "I was just telling them what happened when I went to the bank."

The director glanced at his wristwatch. "At this time of the evening? Is the bank open?"

The young man shook his head. "I hadn't gone for any transaction."

As the director stepped out, he delivered his parting shot: "Then what? To rob it?"

A split second of silence hung in the air, followed by a burst of full-throated laughter. The lift doors closed on the mirth of the men.

That director is my father. In our family, thanks to him, we default to levity. His sense of humor flows in my veins. At every party, he regales the gathering with jokes and mimicry. His wit and charm won people over first, followed closely by his twinkling eyes and a naughty smile.

The epithet, "father's ditto" became attached to my name as I grew. The moment anyone clapped eyes on me, they couldn't help but marvel at how much I resembled my father. I harrumphed at the description – did it mean I looked like a boy? When I whined to my mother, she laughed and gently pointed out that my father had feminine features. She heaved out an old album full of black-and-white photographs of him, handsome with his soft brown eyes, rosebud mouth, and sideburns. It pacified me but only a little.

As a child and even an adolescent, I spent most of my time with my mother, and looked up to her, like I imagine most girls did. The role of provider consumed my father completely, and he could devote little energy to his family, especially his younger daughter. He busied himself with the onerous task of lifting us out of middle-class life, to elevate us to a more comfortable financial position.

Occasionally he took it upon himself to tutor me in Mathematics, but his patience wore out within minutes. Once he rolled up a newspaper and thwacked me on the head when I couldn't solve a sum that he'd set for me. Watching him toil in his office from the time I was ten imbued in me a strong sense of work ethic. I witnessed him putting in long hours at the firm where he worked. His principles and a strong sense of loyalty have embedded themselves deep within my psyche so that I can't fake a sick day even if I wanted to. I often chide him for this trait of mine, but only half-jokingly.

I remember he had once confessed to me he loved his job and expressed a desire to work until his final days. That was not to be, as his firm did not wish to keep him on due to his advancing years. Eight years ago, he retired and moved to live in the same apartment complex as me, albeit two buildings away.

He embarked on the routine of retired life. Every morning he undertook a walk of a minimum of thirty-five minutes. The morning walk gained him immense renown in our neighborhood. All his fellow walkers and our neighbors discovered that come rain or sunshine, my father would be there circling the buildings, often carrying the newspaper in his hand. He intended to solve the weekly Sunday cryptic crossword during the week, and I often joined him in this pleasurable exercise. We walked at a comfortable pace and filled the minutes with lively banter. We solved fewer clues and squandered precious time in making jokes. Sometimes, we also indulged in the unseemly habits of gossiping and passing comments on our fellow walkers.

The walk tired him out, so he followed it up with reading the newspapers and partaking in a leisurely cup of tea. Doing the chores around the house came naturally to him, and even now he never balks at washing the dishes or putting in the laundry.

Four years ago, when I gave birth to my son, my father took me to the hospital and waited by my side until my husband turned up. My son adores his grandfather more than I can say. They are constant companions, and I think my son regards him more as a friend than a parent figure.

Whenever I needed it, my father stepped in and offered his services to drop my kids at school or pick them up. The kids loved it and demanded that he pick them up rather than me.

One cool night around the end of January this year, my father prodded me awake. He was in pain. We rushed to the hospital and later admitted him. It turned out that he had suffered a partial stroke, which rendered it difficult for him to swallow any kind of food.

For four days, my sister and I looked after him in the hospital. We stuck by his side, but the other thing that never left him was his sense of humor and wit. He charmed over the doctors and nurses that streamed in to keep an eye on him. He returned home in good health and spirits, and to my immense relief, he began to consume food normally within the weeks that followed.

Unfortunately, after the stroke, he had to renounce his favorite morning walks and the chores of dropping my children to and from school. But that matters little to me, and I have taken over his duties joyfully, grateful that he is otherwise healthy and continues to entertain us and even babysit my children when he can.

I have always had and continue to have a good relationship with my father, but his love for my children shone a strong spotlight on it.

REMEMBRANCE

A.V. Cruz
The Bronx, New York

What is a father? Someone who tucks their daughter into bed at night and teaches her to ride a bike? The man who protects her and intimidates her preteen crush on her first date or walks her down the aisle on her wedding day? He who teaches her to drive, to balance a checkbook, and to do her taxes? I don't know. You were gone before most of those milestones.

August 2020 marked the 15th anniversary of your death. I'm flabbergasted when I think about everything in and about my life that you haven't shared. You don't know the flaws and attributes that make up the woman I am. The smiles and tears that have graced my face. None of my closest, oldest friends ever got to meet you. I don't even remember the 13-year-old kid you knew (other than I was a damn brat who had just discovered sarcasm) so what do I talk about in an essay on father-daughter relationships?

Memories? Okay, let's try that. I remember you adored me. Of all your seven children, I was your sore spot. We spent so much of my early childhood together. I'm not sure exactly when you hurt your back working as a Pepsi deliverer and started collecting disability, causing Mom to reenter the workforce and you to stay at home with me. But the copious laughter that emanated from me because of your silly energy still rings in my ears.

I remember your hands. They were big and rough, like unconditioned leather that were forever infused with the smell of weed and Bambu paper. We'd spend hours at the green aluminum-framed chalkboard on the entrance wall of our Bronx apartment playing tic-tac-toe. Your right hand would hold my tiny pale left one as you showed me how to draw grape bunches and middle fingers.

An interesting babysitter, you were. You tried to teach me to throw steak knives into the hardwood floors and make them stick (a talent I never acquired), and to gamble in Cee-Lo and 7-11 games (a talent I did). These weren't skills I would have learned in daycare or preschool but, hey, I didn't die, right?

I mostly remember how ruthlessly honest you were, no matter how young I was. Like every time we'd watch my favorite movie, *The Lion King,* you'd explain the concept of death to me while I was belting out "Circle of Life." How it was inevitable. How you wouldn't always be around. Or once, during one of the hundred trips we took to Spanish Harlem, where you grew up after coming from Puerto Rico, you saw me staring at a strung-out old woman. She stood next to the entrance of the bodega we were leaving, swaying like leaves in a summer breeze. Her eyes were closed and her mouth agape. I remember thinking she was asleep, and I asked you how she could do that standing up.

"She's not sleeping, Flaca," you said gruffly as you pulled me in the direction of your car. "She's high on heroin."

"What's that?" You answered in *detail*. And during the ride home—and on many occasions afterward— you described different drugs, their highs, their lows. You told me that you had been addicted to heroin a long, long time ago, before I was born. That the red juice in the little plastic bottles you always had around was methadone, the medicine for the addiction.

Your honesty, I think, helped me cope with the suddenness of your death. That summer in 2005 is still a blur. Our weekly visits to Playland Park turned into daily hospital visits. I understood that the hepatitis C you had contracted from your intravenous drug use had morphed into liver cancer, which had already metastasized and spread through your whole body. It doesn't matter that I don't recall how much time the doctors speculated you had because you only lasted three weeks after the diagnosis. In that time, we went from eating arroz con gandules together to me barely being able to spoon watermelon into your mouth to you lying comatose in a hospital bed. It was as you said. You wouldn't always be here. And then you weren't.

As I think about that summer and the ones that followed, nostalgia pumps out of my heart then circulates yearning through my veins. I try to imagine if you were still here. How could you have shaped my adolescence and emergence into adulthood? I think we would still have been close through my teen years. I can see our frequent shopping trips to Bay Plaza mall, buying clothes at JCPenney, and eating lunch at Applebee's. You would have helped me with my Spanish homework, and I'd be fluent in the language today. Our conversations would have become less one-sided as I'd gotten older, and I would have been able to have more tangible opinions about history and music and life. Or maybe they'd have stayed one-sided because you would have been an old man by then and I'd have felt misunderstood by you. I don't even want to think about how the sex talk would go. I still cringe at the memory of you talking to me about your erectile dysfunction when I was eight, and how you had to "get it fixed so it can work for your mother."

My imagination runs out when I try to envision our relationship as two full adults, as equals. During childhood and adolescence, the father is still an authority, no matter how close the relationship. But after that, when you and I, the parent, and the offspring, would be on the same level of life, I'm lost on how the dynamic might be. And it's because I can't know you at this stage in life. I can only learn from you and try to analyze the information on my own.

For instance, I was in my early twenties when I learned that you used to abuse Mom. It was late one weekend night, and after lots of whiskey and beer, Jay and Amanda were recalling some of the fights that ended in violence. I don't know if I hid my shock well or if they were too inebriated to notice, but I sat there, immobile, unable to compute the details in my head. Flashes of ugly arguments that I wedged my tiny four-year-old self between to referee streaked across my inner sight. I thought, "Dad did that? Did those hands that washed chalk residue from my fingers bruised my mother's body? The hands that fed me boiled bacalao with olive oil drizzled on top harmed her?" In later sober days, I'd try to work out the reasons why you'd stoop to such actions.

And what I wanted most was to confront you about it. To hear… what? Your reasoning? Your remorse? Stories from your childhood and upbringing that justified of those actions. But I couldn't confront you. I had to rely on researched statistics for domestic abuse and memoirs by survivors to try to answer the questions I burned to ask you. Quietly and alone, I had to reprocess all that I knew about you. I had to analyze all the different aspects of your relationship with Mom and come up with an opinion that wouldn't completely smear your memory or villainize me for still loving and missing you. But I can't help but wonder, how would our relationship have changed if I were able to confront you about it?

It's a confusing feeling that the same factor that restricts me from imagining an adult bond with you is also what makes me miss you the most. I could have benefitted from all those adult conversations so much more now that life has fucked me royally a time or two. I need so many of the conversations that you didn't have the chance to drill into my conscience that might save me from stupid mistakes or regrets. My siblings, Jay, and Amanda especially, stepped in as parents and I don't even want to know who I'd be without them. They've imparted a lot of your wisdom to me and given me enough insight into who you were that I can construct any sort of kinship with you. I think you would be proud of us.

And in the future, I'll imagine you with me at all the milestones as I have since you passed. All future birthdays and housewarmings, you'll be there toasting me. If I have children of my own, I'll squeeze orange juice straight from the fruit into their mouths as you did to me. I'll always hum *"Under the Boardwalk"* every time I go to the beach as you did. And I'll always love you. No matter what.

ABOUT THE CONTRIBUTORS

Janeth A. Benjamin is a freelance writer, poet and author living in the Bronx, New York. She has two published poetry collections, *Bloom by 30, The Miki Chronicles* and *April Showers*. She considers herself a storyteller and through her poetry she hopes to inspire and motivate her readers to find themselves through rediscovery and reflection. Also, to practice self-care, through acceptance, self-awareness, and gratitude and to authentically show up for themselves every single day. To build and maintain a strong relationship with God through faith and surrender. You can follow Janeth on Instagram @themikichronicles.

Cher Finver is a mother, wife, writer, and motivational speaker living in Las Vegas, NV. She has published several works of fiction and nonfiction and is the author of the 2017 memoir, But You Look So Good and Other Lies.

Eleanor Sevigny resides in Galesburg, Illinois. She has a BA in Creative Writing from Knox College. Eleanor is a stay-at-home mom to two daughters. In addition to caring for her two children, Eleanor works for The Burg newspaper and is a freelance writer

Natalie Carroll is from Hartlepool England but lives in Scotland. She was first published at the age of 14 and has since been published in other anthologies. Her goal is to have her own work published. Her inspirations are Carol Ann Duffy, Edgar Allan Poe, John Green, JK Rowling, and many more literary greats.

MacKenzie Miller was born and raised in Portland, Oregon. She currently writes for two online music publications, The Cheetah Press and Soft Sound Press, dissecting some of her favorite music. She spends her free time either behind a computer as a writer or behind a camera as a photographer. This is her first publication in print.

Dianne R. Scott is the proud mother of two beautiful children, the second sibling of five incredible women born to two wonderful parents, and an auntie to six extraordinary nieces and nephews. Born and raised in Delaware, she continues to reside there in the city of Dover. After medically retiring from an administrative career at the local state university due to the progressive perils of Multiple Sclerosis (MS), Dianne began to pursue her interest in freelance writing. Her articles relative to societal and current events have appeared in local newspapers. Also, at present, she moderates an online MS community and is a contributor/author for an online publication. This will be the first anthology in which she will be a contributor and she is in the process of writing her book, Sunny with A Chance Of MS.

Dr. Archana Bahadur Zutshi is an Indian poet, author, and translator. She has two published volumes of poetry. 'Poetic Candour' is her debut collection of poetry (2018) and 'The Speaking Muse,' (2019), both available on Amazon. Her Ph.D. research is on the poetry of Philip Larkin and Nissim Ezekiel. A teacher by profession, she is a translator and author of chapters in literary texts. An accomplished poet winning in several contests. She has won prizes and has been a poetry judge for On Fire, the Cultural Movement, and United by Ink.

She is a contributing poet in several anthologies (The Kali Project: Invoking the Goddess Within, Anthologies by Poetry Planet and The Poet House, UK), Essence of Woman (a coffee table book), journals, and blogs. Her poetry was featured by 'Culturium' (March 18, 2019) on Women's Day and Poetry Day. 'Poetic Candour' features in Culturium's collection. Some of her poems are published in All Poetry, United by Ink, Spillwords, Confluence, Setu, The Bilingual Journal, The Madras Courier, MirrorSpeak, Duotrope Poetry Blog, On Fire Cultural Movement, My Words: A Renaissance, Poetry Planet, etc

In the Indian Journal of Comparative Literature and Translation Studies, her translated poems of Nirala were published. Her detailed scholastic interviews have appeared in print by The Poet Magazine (UK), 21st Century Critical Thought Volume 2 (India), and her views on social thought at audiovisual news portal Hungama Times. The Speaking Muse has been featured in The Asian Extract, a print Magazine. She translated a novel on Meerabai from Hindi to English, available on Kindle and Amazon, – 'Meerabai the Legend: Her Life and Struggle as a Woman' (Sudhakar Adeeb).

Aeriel Matthews, is a Christian blogger and author, sexual abuse survivor, youth bible study, and character development teacher from Maple Hill, NC. She received her B.S. in biology from Winston Salem State University. After graduating with a B.A. in biology, she went on to fulfill her call as a youth minister. In that time, she created the first & only youth bible study in her hometown area and has spoken at several youth conferences, teaching youth the importance of Christ. She currently works as a medical laboratory scientist and continues her ministry through her weekly blog at www.aerielwynnell.com, in the publishing of her first book: "Growing Pains" and her YouTube channel.

Lea Vida Reyes Del Moro is from the Philippines; she is an elementary teacher and worked as a freelance contributor writer in different online publications. Her inspirations are JK Rowling, Nicholas Sparks, Paulo Coelho, Stephenie Meyer, Stephen King, Neil Shusterman, and many more literary greats.

Shatara S. Clark, known to most as "TyTalks" is the founder of TyTalks, a non-profit organization that aims to empower women through writing, public speaking, and Bible Study fellowship. Aside from being a high school educator for over 8 years, she is an author of three books: an e-book for the recently single woman titled The Playbook, a paperback devotional for all ages on navigating life titled Sturdy by 30, and a memoir of her family written with her mother titled Ginny's Girls. She recently took on an additional role as a publisher under her sole proprietorship Ty Writes which has been a blessing in the lives of those desiring to tell their stories and have them published and in the hands of many. Shatara is the leader and founder of the Quiet Strength Bible Study and Ministry which sits under her TyTalks non-profit. Shatara aims to encourage women to learn to submit to and wait on the Lord as we are His bride before anyone else's.

Lois Perch Villemaire, a resident of Annapolis, Maryland, is retired from a career in local government. She now explores her lifelong interest in creative writing, including flash fiction, memoir, and poetry. Lois is enthusiastic about researching family history which at times provides her with colorful and unique writing material. Her work has appeared online and in journals including Potato Soup Journal, Ponder Savant, FewerThan500, The Drabble, Pen-in-Hand, Flora Fiction, North of Oxford, Flash Frontier, and in several anthologies published by Truth Serum Press.

Zoe Fawkes is an American novelist and essayist, as well as a policy analyst and international human rights specialist. She currently teaches political science in Kansas City, having lived, and studied all over the world. She has published theater reviews, historical fiction, erotica, essays, and papers on human trafficking, identity politics, voting rights, and immigrant rights under various names. She spends her current life Zoom-teaching, drinking tea, and snuggling with her whippets.

Dr. Lisa Vermette is an education leader, passionate about igniting the fire of reading and writing in adult learners. She is a writer, photographer, and fierce protector of the Humanities, using mixed media to explore important topics of the day. Her social documentary work includes "Fallen Through the Cracks: Raising Awareness about 14 million Illiterate Americans" and "Out of the Shadows: Human Trafficking in Maine: visual and performing arts performance". You can see some of her work: https://theartofmaine.wordpress.com/ or follow her on instagram@ theart_ofmaine.

Melissa Siig is an award-winning journalist and editor based in Tahoe City, California. Her articles have appeared in Nevada Magazine, ESPN.com, Alaska Airlines Magazine, the Reno-Gazette Journal, and SKIING. Her story, "Tahoe Magic," was published in 2012 in the anthology "Tahoe Blues" (Bona Fide Books). An excerpt from her memoir, "The Scud Missile," was published in 2020 in Beyond Words Literary Magazine, and another excerpt,

"Baggage," in November in Gold Man Review. When not writing articles or working on her memoir "All of Our Goodbyes Are Yours," Melissa is busy wrangling her three children and large German shepherd and running a one-screen movie theater she owns with her husband.

Tara Conrad, MFA lives in Pennsylvania with her husband, their four young adult children, and a variety of pets. Her short story Innocence Lost, Courage Found is her most recent publication. In addition to writing, Tara loves editing and hopes to do more of that in the future. Tara mainly writes romance novels where she shares her love of the BDSM lifestyle through her characters. She's also the author of the blog Take a Walk on the Wild Side. You can follow her blog and see her upcoming releases on her website www.tlconradauthor.com

Sewit Mesfen is a technical writer; she also writes fiction, non-fiction, and essays. She spent most of her life in Las Vegas, Nevada after spending her childhood years in California. When not writing, she can be found exploring abandoned structures, creating (and subsequently destroying) multimedia art, and finding independent bookstores. You can follow her adventures on Instagram @_weygud.

Julie Isaacson resides in the north suburbs of Chicago, where she is a teacher of Literacy for students of all ages, and a writer of short stories and poetry. She is the author of an anthology entitled Angry Chef: Satisfying Recipes Inspired by Unsatisfying Relationships. Her poems have received awards in a variety of venues, including Highland Park Poetry and Illinois State Poetry Society. She serves on the board of East on Central, Journal of Arts and Letters, where she is a regular contributor. In addition to these passions, Julie also enjoys performing stories in venues in the Chicago area, including Short Story Theatre and This Much is True. She is currently working on a memoir, based upon family life near the Mississippi River. She enjoys exploring creations in the kitchen, playing piano, and long walks with her dog. She looks forward to more travel, particularly to California to visit her adult children.

Michelle Spencer is a published author in various online and print publications. She often writes about her family and the musings in our world. She wrote a column called "Out of the Mouth of Dad" housed in the Good Men Project in which Michelle shares stories and adventures of her and her filter less father, and their adventures. Michelle has worked in healthcare for over thirty years on the patient side and has spent the last ten years in patient advocacy. Her passion is working with medical residents on communication and difficult conversations. She hosts a podcast called Healthcare Communication Solutions where she interviews clinicians from across the globe on best practices to effectively strengthen the patient-doctor relationship through communication. These conversations are directed to medical residents, fellows, or seasoned physicians looking for strategies to better communicate with their patients.

Her website is www.healthcarecommunicationsolutions.com and she welcomes any comments and feedback. Michelle has four beautiful children and a wonderful husband who encourages and supports her to follow her dreams and keep writing!

Wendy Toth Notarnicola is a freelance writer and editor from Long Valley, New Jersey. She especially enjoys writing haiku and short stories, and her work has been accepted for publication in several journals, including Everyday Fiction, Wales Haiku Journal, Presence, Poetry Pea, Frogpond, Hedgerow, and several anthologies. She received an honorable mention from the 34. Annual Cherry Blossom/Sakura Festival Haiku Contest and is a finalist in the 31. Ito En Oi Ocha Shin haiku Contest, Japan.

Ya'el Chaikind, MPH, MA, LPCC is a published author and poet, including seven books and numerous poems, essays, short stories, and articles. As a licensed psychotherapist, she supports clients in re-writing the stories that no longer serve them to create a life of more connection, meaning, and belonging. Over the past 20 years, she has assisted clients in writing books and memoirs, publicly performed as a storyteller and poet, and offered writing workshops around the U.S. She lives in beautiful Santa Fe, NM.

A.V. Cruz is a new writer from the Bronx. Her fiction explores the dark, gritty side of experiences and symbols that we often see represented as romantic feminine ideals. She is a proud fur-mom who is always ready to talk about books and food.

Jenny Nash is a non-binary photographer and curator, born in Yorkshire in the North of England. Nash began as a documentary and protest photographer which has taken them all over the UK to document specifically LGBTQ+ Pride and their work with Stand Up To Racism. Since 2018 this photographer has taken part in 25 exhibitions in the UK and internationally, has been featured in 18 magazines, and published in 4 books. Jenny Nash won the Leyden Gallery Emerging Artist award in 2020 and 2021 was shortlisted for the New Emergence Art Prize. Nash currently organizes and hosts Photography talks for London Independent Photography whilst organizing and curating group exhibitions in London.

Gargi Mehra works as a Project Manager in the IT arm of an international bank. Her work has appeared in numerous literary magazines online and in print, including The Forge Literary Magazine, The Temz Review, The Writer, and others. She lives in Pune, India with her husband and two children. She blogs at www.gargimehra.com.

www.ingramcontent.com/pod-product-compliance
Lightning Source LLC
Chambersburg PA
CBHW071332150726
47997CB00002B/695